COMPLETE LIST OF GAMES INCLUDED

1942: Pacific Air War
1944: Across the Rhine
ABM Command
Adventures of MicroMan
Alone in the Dark
Alone in the Dark II
Amnesia
Atlantic City Blackjack
Backgammon
Bago
Bandit
Battle Chess CD-ROM
Battle Chess 4000
Battles in Distant Deserts
Battles on Distant Planets
Blackthorne
Blake Stone
Bow & Arrow
Brainteaser
BreakThru
Canfield for Windows
Casino Twenty-One
Castle of the Winds
Castles 2
Cipher for Windows
Civilization
Civilization Editor
Corridor 7: Alien Invasion
Crime Trivia
Crime Patrol
Cyclones
Dark Legions
David Leadbetter's Greens
Day of the Tentacle
Destroyer for Windows
Detroit
Dominate
Doom
Doom: DeHackEd
DoomCAD
DoomEd: The Real Thing
Bonus! Doom Levels and Patches
Double Match

DragonSphere
Draw 5 Video Poker
Empipe
Empire Deluxe
Bonus! Empire Deluxe Scenarios
The Elder Scrolls 1: Arena
Empire II for Windows
F-15 Strike Eagle III
Falcon 3.0/Falcon Gold
Flashback
Freddy Pharkas
Front Page Sports: Baseball
Gabriel Knight
GNU Chess
GopherIt!
Gunship 2000
Halloween Harry
Hangem
Hexxagon
IGO
Indiana Jones & the Fate of Atlantis
Invasion of the Mutant Space Bats
of Doom
Jetpack
Bonus! Jetpack Levels
Jill of the Jungle
Jpuzzle
Kiloblaster
Lode Runner: The Legend Returns
Bonus! Lode Runner Levels
The Lost Vikings
Mah Jongg
Master of Orion
Master of Magic
MechWarrior 2: The Clans
MegaTron
Menzoberranzan
Millenium Auction
Ms. Chomp
Myst
Mystic Towers
Out of this World
Pentominos

Pinball Fantasies
Prairie Dog Hunt
Prairie Dog Hunt II
Quattra Command
Railroad Tycoon Deluxe
Raptor
Ravenloft
Rebel Assault
Return to Zork
Runner
Sam 'n' Max Hit the Road
Shadowcaster
SimCity 2000
Bonus! SimCities
Solar Winds
Space Pirates
Spear of Destiny
Spectre VR
Spider Solitaire
Spin 'n' Win
Star Trek: 25th Anniversary
Star Trek: Judgment Rites
Stellar Warrior
SubWar 2050
System Shock
Terminator: Rampage
Theme Park
TIE Fighter
TurboGo
Ultima Underworld
Ultimate NFL Football
Voodoo Doll for Windows
Watch Out Willi!
Windows Video Poker
WinFight
WinRisk
World Circuit
World War II Battles
X-COM
X-Wing
Xatax
Zone 66

For Every Kind of Computer User, There is a Sybex Book.

All computer users learn in their own way. Some need straightforward and methodical explanations. Others are just too busy for this approach. But no matter what camp you fall into, SYBEX has a book that can help you get the most out of your computer and computer software while learning at your own pace.

Beginners generally want to start at the beginning. The **ABC's** series, with its step-by-step lessons in plain language, helps you build basic skills quickly. For a more personal approach, there's the **Murphy's Laws** and **Guided Tour** series. Or you might try our **Quick & Easy** series, the friendly, full-color guide, with **Quick & Easy References**, the companion pocket references to the **Quick & Easy** series. If you learn best by doing rather than reading, find out about the **Hands-On Live!** series, our new interactive multimedia training software. For hardware novices, there's the **Your First** series.

The **Mastering and Understanding** series will tell you everything you need to know about a subject. They're perfect for intermediate and advanced computer users, yet they don't make the mistake of leaving beginners behind. Add one of our **Instant References** and you'll have more than enough help when you have a question about your computer software. You may even want to check into our **Secrets & Solutions** series.

SYBEX even offers special titles on subjects that don't neatly fit a category—like our **Pushbutton Guides**, our books about the Internet, our books about the latest computer games, and a wide range of books for Macintosh computers and software.

SYBEX books are written by authors who are expert in their subjects. In fact, many make their living as professionals, consultants or teachers in the field of computer software. And their manuscripts are thoroughly reviewed by our technical and editorial staff for accuracy and ease-of-use.

So when you want answers about computers or any popular software package, just help yourself to SYBEX.

For a complete catalog of our publications, please write:

SYBEX Inc.
2021 Challenger Drive
Alameda, CA 94501
Tel: (510) 523-8233/(800) 227-2346 Telex: 336311
Fax: (510) 523-2373

TALK TO SYBEX ONLINE.

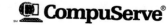

Tom McDonald's

PC GAMES
EXTRAVAGANZA!

T. LIAM McDONALD

SYBEX®

SAN FRANCISCO
PARIS
DÜSSELDORF
SOEST

Acquisitions Editor: Kristine Plachy

Developmental Editor: Gary Masters

Editor: Michelle Khazai

Technical Editor: Frank Seidel

Book Designer: Elizabeth McDonald

Contributing Editor: Colin Williamson

Desktop Publisher: Elizabeth McDonald, An EMC² Production

Screen Graphics: Al Packer

Production Assistant: Marc Duro

Technical Support: Erik Ingenito

Indexer: Matthew Spence

Cover Designer: Archer Design

Cover Illustrator: Mike Miller

Game Gurus: Matt Firme and Stephen Poole

Library of Congress Card Number: 94-74084

ISBN: 0-7821-1654-X

Manufactured in the United States of America

10 9 8 7 6 5 4 3 2 1

For
John David Gray
and
Helen Gray
who meant the world to me

One half of the world does not understand
the pleasures of the other.
Jane Austen

X

ACKNOWLEDGMENTS

As a Contributing Editor to *PC Gamer*, *CD-ROM Today*, and *Computer Entertainment News*, I've had the pleasure of working with some of the fine people at GP Publications. Steve Poole, Matt Firme, Lance Elko, Selby Bateman, and the rest are just a few of the good guys involved in the gaming business. If you want to see some of the best computer reporting in the field, bar none, check out these magazines. *PC Gamer* and *CD-ROM Today* in particular come with a CD in every issue, and they're packed with useful stuff.

Once again, this book was Gary Masters' idea. My thanks to him for thinking of me to write it, and for massaging my ego by putting my name above the title (which was also his idea). My editor, Michelle Khazai, did a terrific job, and needs to be commended simply for having to deal with me. Countless lives were no doubt saved by Michelle's intervention. Erik Ingenito provided valuable technical input at some pretty dire moments.

I had some help in writing some of these entries, particularly from Colin Williamson, who wrote about *Alone in the Dark*, *Sam and Max Hit the Road*, *Day of the Tentacle*, *The Lost Vikings*, *Mystic Towers*, and *Star Trek* for me. Thanks for the fine work!

Sony was gracious enough to provide me with their beautiful Trinitron Multiscan 17sf monitor for putting this book together, and I'm grateful to them for their generosity, and to Jennifer San Dretto of Technology Solutions for helping arrange it.

Creative Labs provided their top-of-the-line Soundblaster 16 multimedia kit, an AWE 32 board, and the Video Blaster RT300 for my use, and I'd like to thank Theresa Pulido for getting these to me. Thanks also to Christine Kohlstedt of Pat Meier Associates for getting me the Advanced Gravis Ultrasound Max board. To make all that sound really come together, I had the good fortune of getting hold of Altec/Lansing's full speaker setup, which really rocks. Just put that subwoofer up against your desk, crank the bass, and feel the whole room vibrate.

Cathy Panos, and now Alison Evans, from CH Products have always gotten me the latest in flight peripherals, and I swear by their amazing CH Flightstick Pro. (Thrustmaster *wishes* it was this good.)

Thus ends the shameless plugs section.

My thanks also go to the numerous companies and press representatives who have helped me not only with this book, but throughout my years as a journalist covering this industry. Dany Brooks and Marcia Galea of Electronic Arts, Holly Hartz and the gang at Spectrum HoloByte (they throw a mean party, and don't even water down the drinks!), Paula Rebich of MicroProse, Sue Seserman and Camilla Boswell of Lucas-Arts, Galen Svanas and David Swofford of Origin Systems, Mike Lustenberger of New World Computing, Jay Wilbur of id, April Souza of SSI, Kathy Gilmore and Maureen McNulty Smith of Sierra On-Line, Bill Linn of the ImagiNation Network, Monica Rae Pierce of Interplay, Carl Norman, late of 360 Pacific and now with SSI, Suzanne Nelson and Sally Vandershaf of Maxis, Tony Pannachio of Capstone, James Yakoto and the TriloByte folks, Paul Baldwin of Domark, Chris Foster and Lisa Petrocchi of Impressions, Keith Zabalaoui of Atomic Games, Rina Jackson and Kathleen Burke of Broderbund, Maria Atake of I-Motion, Melissa Bigwin of Bethesda Softworks, and Roger Smith of the American Go Association, as well as people at Techology Solutions, Pat Meier Associates, Golin-Harris, Waggener Edstrom, Killer Apps, and Criswell Communications, are just a few of the folks who make my job easier.

Of course, the shareware developers and publishers deserve an incredible amount of praise. These are people who work almost completely out of love and the mere chance of renumeration. Without them, this book would be much poorer, and I thank them one and all for their fine work in a tough field. They're working for your entertainment, folks, so do them a favor and *register your shareware*! There are no excuses not to.

My buddies Matt Costello, Rick Hautala, Charlie Grant, Chet Williamson, Gary Chapin, and Tom Monteleone continue to offer valuable feedback in all areas related to computers, games, hardware, and life. Bernie Yee, Bill Trotter, Tom "K.C." Basham, Lee Buchanan, Neil Randall, Ed Dille, Trent Ward, and David Wade are just a few of the writers out here in the trenches covering this ever-growing field, and I've always appreciated their insights and the time they take to offer them.

My wife Elizabeth displayed infinite patience, love, and understanding throughout this sometimes trying project. Her company, EMC^2, also did a bang-up job on the design and layout. My parents have always been supportive, and helped out this time with a loan to buy a Pentium when my system crapped out midway through this book. Thanks also to my brothers Matt and John and their families; Rich and Anne Marie Redmon, for their computer support and hospitality; Laurens Schwartz, for being a terrific agent and lawyer; and Godzilla, for being there.

Anyone with any comments, questions, or hate mail can contact me on CompuServe either in the Sybex Forum (GO SYBEX) or at 71042,3134. I'll try to field tech questions where possible.

TABLE OF CONTENTS

XIV

TWO
Classics, Cards, Puzzles, & Sports Games   69

THREE
Role Playing and Adventure Games   **109**

XVIII

INTRODUCTION

INTERACTIVE ENTERTAINMENT NOW

The countdown has begun. The final moments of the twentieth century are already clicking away, and the clock seems to race faster each year. We are moving forward into an unknown and unknowable future, and it's going to be here long before we're ready for it. And, as motion pictures helped shape society at the beginning of this century, and television did at its mid-point, so will interactive entertainment be a force for change in this new millennium.

The past years have seen an unprecedented acceleration in the development of new and better technologies. Computer technology in particular has made astonishing, and some might say frightening, inroads into everyday life, and not a single area of our professional and personal lives remains unaffected by it. We know where this technology is right now, and have an idea of where it is going, but no one is really sure how it will change us. One thing is certain, however: it *will* change us.

We created these machines to help us. To make us more productive. To help launch us into new areas of discovery and invention. They've done that, and will continue to, but we always knew there was something more they could do. The last technological revolution humanity experienced was one of transportation, and the development of new transportation types such as the automobile and airplane affected every area of industry, commerce, and warfare. But they also reached the common person, who wanted to use them for pleasure and entertainment: a drive in the country, a vacation in a far-away land.

So it is with computers. The earliest hackers were barely finished with their "real work" for the day when they began making rudimentary computer games using crude graphics created by standard characters and type symbols. If computers had only ever offered increased productivity, they would never have penetrated the consumer market as they have. It's a simple fact which many want to ignore or dismiss, but it's unassailable: *without entertainment products, there would have been no home computer revolution.* Therefore, computers would have been slower to develop and people would have taken longer to adapt to them. This, of course, would have impacted on the productivity computers offer the marketplace.

As it is, millions of American homes now have some kind of PC. Children take to them with an almost frightening ease, and they're not doing it so they can run *Lotus 1-2-3*: like all of us, they want to play. Now more people are playing, and more people will continue to play as this technology becomes cheaper and more readily available. Every indicator is pointing to a future where television and movies are interactive, where virtual reality is as near as the closest mall, or maybe right there in your living room.

But that's no surprise to computer gamers: we knew it all along.

I guess you could call it The Revenge of the Computer Game Geeks. We spent years with flight simulators, role-playing games, arcade shooters, and enough bleary-eyed hours with *Civilization* alone to make friends and spouses doubt our sanity. But in 1994, it was suddenly all the rage, and we had our quietly smug moment of self-satisfaction. You can barely open a magazine or turn on CNN without the words *interactive entertainment*, *virtual reality*, *information super-highway*, or even *CD-ROM* throttling you. Everyone is abuzz with the possibilities, and the media pundits are screaming "wave of the future" so loudly that they can't even hear us say "We told you so."

They're learning what computer gamers always knew: that the passive existence of the television-watching couch spud is the slow road to mental oblivion. Computer games may be mindless entertainment, but at least they aren't *passive* mindless entertainment. The mind is set to work at a task, be it a puzzle or controlling an airplane or merely killing something. The imagination is engaged, and a world that did not exist before rises before the user. This world is the user's to explore and challenge, to shape or conquer.

Imagine the possibilities! In one compact machine, taking up less space, in some cases, than a large book, you can become a dogfighting ace in World War I, a princess in a fantasy realm, a hero on a quest to slay a dragon, a high-stakes gambler, a pirate, a general, or lord of the world. These games can transport you from medieval England to the far reaches of space. They can take you places you have never been before, and put you in control. They challenge, and entertain, and even sometimes educate. They are the playgrounds of the imagination and the intellect. They are, simply, fun.

And they're here to stay.

WELCOME

I'm here to give you a brief tour of this brave new world via some 130-odd games, and another couple-hundred add-ons. You can consider these games as representative of the best of a large sector of the gaming market. (For space reasons, I decided to exclude kids' games and all but a few sports title, which will appear in Volume II next year.) Each entry in the book is accompanied by a demo or piece of shareware on the CD-ROM.

The idea behind *Tom McDonald's PC Games Extravaganza* is for you to read about a game and give it a test drive to help you decide if you want to buy it. Toward that end, I have included all pertinent information on each title: who made it, where to find it, how to use it, what exactly is on the CD-ROM, how much the game retails for, and where to order it. The intent was to sort through all the titles available at press time and cull those that stand out for one reason or another. If I didn't like the game for some reason, it simply wasn't included. Why bother wasting space with garbage?

So, the criteria was simple. Each game had to:

1. Be notable in its category.

2. Offer something unique or engaging.

3. Have some form of "test-drive" available, such as a demo or shareware.

4. Not suck.

Now, if we had wanted to just fill space, there were plenty of titles with demos that could have been included. Heck, some titles that were excluded even had some admirers. *Spaceship Warlock* springs immediately to mind.

But I hated *Spaceship Warlock*. Playing it was about as pleasant as having an earwig burrow through your brain. *Darkseed* and *CyberRace* are two other pieces of flotsam that were jettisoned early on. Countless others fell by the wayside as I searched for noteworthy software. There is definitely more junk than good stuff out there, but that doesn't mean there isn't plenty of good stuff. And a lot of it came from unknown shareware developers.

Shareware Versus Commercial Titles

At this point, some of you may have already flipped through this book and come to some rudimentary piece of shareware with mediocre graphics and simplistic gameplay. You're saying, "C'mon, how can major titles like *Spaceship Warlock* and *CyberRace* be inferior to *Bago* or *Watch Out Willi!*"

All right, let's look at this question. I'll be honest, and I hope the shareware developers will be too. You simply can't judge a lot of shareware by the criteria you judge mainstream titles by. Most shareware is made by one programmer working alone. There are exceptions, of course, such as *Doom*, *Raptor*, and other high-end shareware. But for the majority, these are simple games with simple graphics and play. They're often not "sexy" or even sophisticated.

But you know what? A lot of them are fundamentally better than games produced by major companies. I would argue that a bare-bones title like *Bago* is more engaging and challenging than an utter mindsucker like *CHAOS Continuum*, or that *Watch Out Willi* has more interesting gameplay than a high-profile waste of time like *Comanche: Maximum Overkill*.

Really take a look at some of this shareware. Some of them are so simple they're actually elegant. Most take up very little hard drive space and require little memory to run. For a quick diversion from work, they're perfect. They're the sleek, featherweight boxer with the finesse and grace to dance around the muscle-bound heavyweight. Without them, computer gaming would be much poorer, and we should be grateful to the independent hackers who give them to us. They're out there on the front lines, in the trenches, making games for the best possible reason: for the sheer love and pleasure of it. And that's the best reason of all.

But Wait! There's More!

Not only have we included demos and shareware, but there are also over 200 "add-ins" for the games you already own! These files can often be found in a subdirectory of the demo or program, and include some real treats. Throughout this book you'll find:

- four dozen new *Doom* levels
- *Doom* editors and a level randomizer
- *Doom* level maps
- several dozen *JetPack* levels
- one hundred *Lode Runner: The Legend Returns* levels
- five *Empire Deluxe* scenarios

- an *X-Wing* game editor
- nine or ten new SimCities for *SimCity 2000*

You'll even find numerous hints, cheat codes, playing strategies and tips scattered throughout the book. Heck, I even did a few pieces about what kind of monkeyshines some of these companies were up to this past year. Now is that a value-packed book or what?!

SOME THINGS YOU SHOULD KNOW

Okay, so that's what you'll find in this here little book. But there are some things you should know, and some rules to playing this game. The first rule is the most important, and that is:

THERE ARE NO FREE LUNCHES!

By buying this book *you have most certainly not bought the rights to the programs on this disc, nor have you purchased technical support for these programs.* This is crucial, since the disc contains numerous fully functional shareware games. If you enjoy and continue playing one of these games you *must register it with the author.* If you don't, the law is quite clear: *you're committing a theft.* It might not seem that way, but you are, and you're hurting an industry that's giving you some enjoyment. So, just send in your money or *stop using the program!*

Unless stated otherwise (i.e.: "freeware" or "public domain"), these are copyrighted programs which the author has released to the public on a *trial basis,* as defined in the author's documentation or message screens. If you like it, register it. Registration entitles you to complete use of the program in question and often additional perks, such as new levels and updates. These vendors will only provide technical support to registered users. The major companies which produced the demos on this disc also only offer support for registered users of their products.

Please help keep the shareware concept alive and register all shareware you find useful on this disc. If *CD Games Extravaganza* inspires you to register a piece of shareware or buy a retail title, please let the company know upon registration.

The Shareware Concept

Shareware (also known as user supported software) is a radical concept in marketing and distribution that is not wholly understood by everyone. The authors of shareware retain all rights to the software under the copyright laws while still allowing free distribution of their product. This gives users the chance to freely obtain and try out software to see if it fits their needs. Shareware should not be confused with "public domain" software even though they are often obtained from the same sources. Public domain software is free, shareware is not.

If you continue to use shareware after trying it out, you are expected to register your use with the author and pay a registration fee. What you get in return depends on the author, but may include a printed manual, free updates, telephone support, and so on. Only by paying for the shareware you use do you enable shareware authors to continue to support their software and create new programs.

Everyone wins with shareware. You get to try out software to make sure it works with your system and that it's something you actually want to buy. The author saves the expense of advertising, packaging and distribution, which drives retail prices up. These savings are passed on to you with lower costs than commercial software.

Shareware and Software Violations

As with all products and trade, there are bound to be violations of copyright, trademark, distribution, and licensing. Shareware violations can be reported to the Association of Shareware Professionals, 545 Grover Road, Muskegon, MI 49442.

Software piracy is another problem, and if you learn of any instances of it, you should report it to the Software Publishing Association, 1730 M Street NW, Suite 700, Washington, DC 20036, (800) 388-7478.

A Note to Shareware Developers

I made every attempt to get in touch with the authors of the work featured in this book. Sometimes we couldn't even tell who was responsible for certain things (this was especially true in regard to *DOOM* levels and similar add-ins). If you're a developer, publisher, or shareware author whose work is featured in this book, or who would like his or her work featured in future volumes of this series, feel free to contact me via CompuServe 71042,3134 or GEnie T.MCDONALD1, or c/o SYBEX Inc., 2021 Challenger Drive, Alameda, CA 94501. I'm on your side, and will do everything I can to provide a proper forum and showcase for your creations.

RUNNING THE GAMES

I've done everything in my power to make sure these are functional, working programs, but be warned: *there will be some computers that just won't run some programs!* I compiled this disc myself, and had no trouble with any program. People with a properly-configured 386/40 with 8 megabytes of RAM, SVGA video card, and Microsoft-compatible mouse should have few problems except for the high end titles like *Myst* or *Rebel Assault*. Please remember, however, that demos are demos: they *will* have bugs and they *will* crash at times. We don't make any claims to or for these programs and, unfortunately, can't offer any technical support.

SYBEX Inc. makes no claims to the programs on this disc, and all copyright, trademark, and other proprietary elements of these programs remain vested with the developers and publishers. Those developers and publishers continue to hold all rights to their programs, demos, and other materials, and those items are not the property of SYBEX Inc. or any of the readers of *PC Games Extravaganza*. The shareware programs and demos included here are the property of their respective owners, and are subject to the guidelines and legal regulations relating to these programs.

What You Get

Several types of programs are placed on this disc. These types are:

• Non-interactive demos of commercial releases.

• Interactive demos of commercial releases.

• Shareware, which must be registered.

• Freeware, or Public Domain software.

These are divided into three main directories. Each file will usually have a name similar to the name of the game.

DOSDEMO contains all DOS demos, both interactive and non-interactive. Look for *.EXE or *.BAT files and enter that name to run.

DOSHARE contains all DOS shareware. Look for *.EXE or *.BAT files and enter that name to run.

WINGAMES contains all Windows demos *and* shareware. These must be run from Windows. Use the File Manager to access the directory and then double-click the *.EXE file to run.

I try to provide accurate information on each title in the accompanying entries found in the book. Their designations, run commands, and directories should be pretty clear. If you're interested in buying a piece of shareware, go to the directory for that program and look for CATALOG.EXE, CATALOG.DOC or ORDER.DOC, ORDERFRM.DOC, or some similarly titled file for detailed ordering information. This will included current rates, postage costs, and whether the vendor accepts credit cards.

SOME CONFIGURATION TIPS

Some programs must be run using a boot disk with a special configuration. This means you'll need special configuration files. If you own DOS 6.0 or higher, you can use its special multi-menuing system to create a menu to run different configurations upon boot-up.

Making a Boot Disk

A boot disk is a disk placed in one of your floppy drives that contains all the necessary information for starting up your system. To create a boot disk you must start with a formatted, blank disk. Place it in your floppy drive and then, at the C:\ prompt, type:

```
SYS A:\
```

This copies the IO.SYS, MSDOS.SYS, and COMMAND.COM file to the disk. You must then copy the AUTOEXEC.BAT and CONFIG.SYS files to this disk by typing:

```
COPY AUTOEXEC.BAT  A:\
COPY CONFIG.SYS A:\
```

If your boot drive is other than drive A (such as drive B), then just substitute B for A in the above lines.

Memory Requirements

After making your boot disk, use the DOS editor to change the CONFIG.SYS and AUTOEXEC.BAT files on the floppy disk. (Don't change the originals.) Take out all but the basic necessities for running your system: mouse drivers, CD-ROM drivers, HIMEM.SYS, and so on. If you try to run a game under your normal configuration and get an out-of-memory message, then try using this "clean" boot disk.

Some games may tell you that there's not enough EMS or "expanded" memory. This means that a special driver needs to be loaded so that the computer can access this special memory. The driver is called the EMM386 driver, and is loaded after the HIMEM.SYS. Try adding the following line to your boot disk if the program requires expanded memory:

```
DEVICE=C:\DOS\EMM386.EXE 2048 RAM
```

This will set aside a certain amount of upper memory for expanded memory.

Windows Games

Some Windows games require a set of files in your X:\WINDOWS\SYSTEM directory in order to work. These files are on the CD-ROM in the X:\WINFILES directory. If you're having trouble with a windows title, just copy all of them into the X:\WINDOWS\SYSTEM directory on your hard drive and the program should work.

HOW TO READ AN ENTRY

Each entry contains information on a title in this book in a gray and black box like this one. This information includes:

GAME TITLE

Who's It From? What developer created the game and, in some cases, which company released it.

Where Is It? What root directory are the program files kept in? Access this directory either in Windows or DOS to run the program.

How Do I Use It? This is the "executable" name. In DOS, you switch to the root directory and type this name. In Windows, you open the Run command, then enter the pathname and the executable name, and click "Okay." You can also access the CD-ROM in File Manager, switch to the root directory, and double-click on the executable.

What Do I Get? Some demos and shareware come with a certain number of levels or features, which are described here.

What Am I Missing? In the case of shareware, what perks (besides a clear conscience) and added features come with registration?

How Much? This is pretty straightforward: what's the manufacturer's suggested retail price? Please note, most products can be bought at retail for substantially lower prices. For most shareware I have added in the cost of shipping.

How Do I Order? This is the address and, where possible, the phone number of the publisher.

Classics

You'll also note that some entries come with little stars in the black title bar that look like this:

These are games that I have deemed all-time, super-cool, really really neat-o peachy keen. I'd call them "classics," but that's the name of a chapter in this book, and things might get confusing. Just remember: when you see this symbol, you are in the presence of greatness.

WHO THE HECK IS THIS GUY?

You may be wondering why you should trust me to guide you through the labyrinthine, crowded world of computer games. Well, the answer is: you shouldn't, ha ha.

Seriously, though, I'm the one who picked the games that went into this book and, more importantly, the ones that didn't. The only reason they're here is because I thought they had merit. But why should you trust my opinion?

As a contributing editor and columnist for some of the top gaming and computer magazines on the market, I literally see *every title that is published.* Evaluating games and writing about them is my full-time job. I've played computer games for years: I know what's come before, and what's coming up. I've designed a few games, and know the fundamentals of game design and content. In seeing so many pieces of software a year, you get some sixth sense that allows you to spot a turkey, and that same sense allows you to see something unique and special.

There are some basic criteria in judging games: they should be easy and intuitive to use, they should be challenging but not so challenging they're undefeatable, they should possess some degree of elegance or grace, and most importantly, they should engage the imagination or intellect. They should rise above their medium. Technical achievement is certainly noteworthy. Sound, graphics, music, and so on are important criteria, but not necessarily a deciding factor unless they are so bad that gameplay itself is undermined. The reason technical wizardry is a secondary factor in judging games is because it is so transitory. Anyone who's been in computers some

time can tell you amusing stories about salespeople who told them, back when they were buying that 8088 CPU, that a ten meg hard drive is "far more than they'll ever need" or how wowed they were when games actually started having graphics with *more than two colors*. (My first computer had two colors: black and not-black).

Like everyone, I'm impressed by technical achievement, but the first law of computer gaming is *no bad game with great graphics will hold a user's interest*. With CD-ROM gaming in a full-blown explosion, we are seeing a depressing number of flashy games with utterly abysmal gameplay. Upon seeing games like this I think of Stephen King's description of the film adaptation of *The Shining:* "It's like a big, beautiful Cadillac with no engine."

And with many newer games, that Caddy is up on blocks.

Content is the key to a good game. If you rub off that shiny surface, is there something built solidly under there? Or is it just made of tin?

We're about to look at some 130 games that are not made of tin. Few, if any, will endure for the ages as chess and Go have, but they are examples of some of the finest interactive entertainment that is available now. Each has something to recommend it, even if that something is small and not of particular interest to every gamer.

But I guarantee you one thing: there will be some games, quite a few games, that are of interest to you. There is something here for every taste.

Happy gaming.

T. Liam McDonald
New Jersey, 1994

ONE

ACTION & ARCADE GAMES

C'mon, admit it: you *like* hefting a shotgun, levelling it at the head of a critter from the bowels of hell, and spraying the walls with blood and entrails. It feels...good, or, in the current vernacular, "proactive" or "empowering," possibly even "liberating."

Yeah, that's the ticket: you're liberating his spleen from the rest of his body.

Unlike many other games discussed in this book, arcade games don't teach you anything, don't require classic strategies, and usually don't involve complex problem solving. For the most part, they require keen hand-eye coordination, quick reflexes, and, often, patience. When most people imagine interactive entertainment, it's the first thing they think of: *Sonic the Hedgehog*, *Mortal Kombat*, *Super Mario Brothers*. To many they are solely the domain of children, but then again, any child who plays *Doom* might have a few good nightmares as a result.

Throughout the rest of *Games Extravaganza*, we'll tackle role-playing games that create entire worlds, strategy games that require keen intellect, and games that have endured for centuries, but right now, we're just going to have a lot of mindless fun. In our hyped-up, supercharged, on-the-go, gotta-be-there-yesterday world, mindless fun is supposedly frowned upon. To sit and do something that has no redeeming intellectual, social, or economic value whatsoever seems anathema to many people. "What's the point?" they may ask.

Sit these folks in front of *Doom* or *Raptor* for a few minutes and they'll soon change their tune.

The fact is, humans need to play. All higher primates do. Even congressmen. The point is, arcade-type games may be a conspicuous waste of time, but they're an *entertaining and socially acceptable* conspicuous waste of time, and that's an important distinction. When you come home from the office—or, for many, while you're at the office supposed to be working—it sometimes feels good to just plop down in front of a computer and take out some of those all-too-human frustrations and aggressions on some harmless pixels. After a half-hour or so, the edge is off, you feel a little more relaxed, and you can go back to the real world. (Then again, maybe you stay up all night trying to get to the third level of *Blake Stone*, thereby endangering your marriage, making yourself useless at work, alienating your friends and children, and sucking up oxygen better used by more sentient life forms. Plankton, for instance. But I digress.)

Arcade games—or "shooters," as they're often called—really came into their own this year as adult entertainment. The big news, of course, was *Doom*: a nightmarish excursion into hell featuring extreme violence and scorching action. It was an arcade game made for grownups, and it reached them as no other game ever had. A good chunk of this chapter is going to be dedicated to *Doom*, with special levels, editors, and other helpful doo-dads.

But there was plenty of other hot news this year for arcade fans: *TIE Fighter*, *CyClones*, *MegaRace*, *Rebel Assault*, and others screamed across screens with truly blazing gameplay. Any game that can raise your pulse-rate the way *MegaRace* can or cause you to jump in your seat like *CyClones* does is doing something right.

We've put a whole bunch of these games on our disk for you, many of them shareware or interactive demos with several playable levels. They range from straight shooters to silly little lunch-break specials, from space sims to racing sims, and all manner of sims in between. The one common denominator is action, and plenty of it.

DOOM ☆

Who's It From? id Software

Where Is It? X:\DOSHARE\DOOM

How Do I Use It? Type DOOM at the DOS prompt

What Do I Get? You get one entire level—Knee Deep in the Dead—with over a half dozen floors to traverse.

What Am I Missing? Two even more hellacious levels, with hot new weapons such as the BFG9000 and the Plasma Rifle, and a whole bunch of nasty new monsters.

How Much? $40.00

How Do I Order? id Software, c/o StarPak, P.O. Box 1230, Greeley, CO 80632. (800) IDGAMES.

Nothing that came before prepared the industry for this phenomenon called *Doom*. Its achievements are multiple. First, it came from a tiny company in Texas, where a group of renegade developers had set up shop to make games that *they* wanted to play. Second, it featured gorgeous texture-mapped graphics and dense sound and music. Third, it delved deep into the dark corners of the imagination to deliver the most explicit violence ever shown on computer, and an unremittingly grim and dread-filled landscape. Fourth, and most amazingly, it reached literally millions of people via shareware, a concept generally disdained by the industry at large.

id Software broke every rule in the book, and came away with the hottest title of the year. No one could stop talking about it. Every vendor at the Consumer Electronics Show was using *Doom* to show how well their system ran. Every network was tied up with people playing head-to-head "Deathmatch" games, and eventually it had to be banned at the workplace. *PC Gamer*, where I'm a Contributing Editor, named it the Number 1 game of all time. The mainstream computer industry suddenly rethought what they'd been doing, added more blood-n-guts to their work, and seriously considered shareware as a viable distribution channel. In short, it was the shotgun blast heard 'round the computer gaming world, and though it may seem corny and hyperbolic to say so, gaming will never be the same again.

Just what is *Doom* you may ask?

Doom is simply the ultimate game of first-person murder and mayhem. You don't have to talk to anyone, your inventory management involves nothing more complex than collecting all the weapons, ammo, health, armor, and keys you can find, and there aren't any puzzles to solve. The purpose of *Doom* is as old as humankind itself: *kill or be killed*.

It is sometime in the future, and you play a battle-hardened marine shipped off to the Mars base for assaulting a superior officer. Mars and its moons, Phobos

Available weapons

Ammo for selected weapon

Health

Your character

Armor

Keys

Amount of ammo & total ammo possible

and Deimos, are home to the Union Aerospace Corporation, who have been using the base not only for treatment of nuclear waste, but for odd experiments in inter-dimensional travel. They've been able to send things from one moon to the other, but they haven't had much luck with transporting people: the marines sent through come out the other side insane and violent.

One day, the Mars base receives a frantic message from Phobos saying that *something* is coming through the gates. Then all contact ceases. You and a crack troop of marines take off for Phobos, where you're ordered to stand guard duty while the rest head inside. Shots and screams are heard, and then nothing. With no way to get off the planet and everyone else dead, you decide to head inside and do what damage you can before going down. You have only a pistol and no armor, and the base is made up of numerous levels and buildings. To make things worse, all your buddies are shambling around as well-armed zombies, looking to take a piece out of you. It also appears that the experiments have opened a door and let some *mighty* unpleasant creatures through.

You have to travel throughout the base, picking up health bonuses (blue bottles), medkits ("red cross" packs), armor bonuses (helmets), clips, shotgun shells, new weapons, "keys" (square, colored cards), and other special items, such as...well, you'll find out. Controlling the game is simple using arrow keys, a mouse, or a joystick. You shoot with the ALT key, open doors with the spacebar, pick things up by walking over them, and access the automap with the TAB key. The first-person graphics are the best yet seen in any title, anywhere. The sensation of movement, with the view bobbing up and down as you run along hallways, com-pletely immerses the user in the game world. Dense sound effects mean you can hear enemies coming from far away, and even tell what direction they're coming

DOOM **CHEATS!**

Just type in these codes while playing *Doom* and you'll activate the "cheat mode" in question. (Not all cheats work all the time in all versions.)

- idbehold: Cheat menu: hit the first letter of the cheat you want. This includes:

S	Super Strength ("Berserk" mode)
V	Invulnerability
I	Partial Invisibility
A	Complete level map in Automap
R	Anti-radiation suit (walk unharmed on toxic lakes)
L	Light Amplification Visors (see in the dark)

- iddqd: "Degreeless" mode: makes you indestructible.

- idchoppers: Gives you the chainsaw. Heeee-yaaa!

- idkfa: "Very happy ammo" mode: gives you all ammo, weapons, and keys, as well as 200% armor.

- idclev: Level warping: type in episode and then level number after it, ie, "idclev25" for episode 2 level 5.

- idspispopd: If you're having trouble finding a secret door, just type this and you'll be able to walk through walls.

from. When something suddenly looms up behind you, you may well jump right out of your chair.

Needless to say, a game as hot as *Doom* attracts a near-fanatical following, many of them dedicated to the multiplayer and "Deathmatch" modes. That's right, *Doom* completely supports modem and network play, so you and a bunch of friends can sit down and play together. (The family that slays together...never mind.) In multiplayer mode, you and a buddy can work together to beat a level. You can see each other firing away or twitching in agony as you both take on waves of monsters. Or better yet, you can play in "Deathmatch" mode, in which you both start at opposite ends of a level, each looking to find and kill the other. (The human is the deadliest prey.) With all the new levels uploaded to bulletin boards, many of them "Deathmatch Certified," and head-to-head play, there is literally no limit to *Doom*. And now *Doom II* is in the stores, featuring completely new levels, designs, monsters, and some fiendish surprises from the folks at id.

DOOM **STUFF!**

Doom's success, and its fanatical following, has spawned countless (literally) cheats, hacks, and new levels, expanding on the possibilities of the *Doom* world like no game ever. These hacks are done by fans and come in four major varieties:

- **Editors:** Change single "sprites" (monsters), or an entire level. These are complete game-editing and building programs and require some effort to learn, but there's nothing quite like designing your very own piece of *Doom*. Some of these editors work by building new *.WAD files, creating a new level-data file for the game, while others edit the information in the DOOM.EXE file itself.

- **Patches:** A patch is something installed on top of *Doom* which changes key features automatically. They range from a monster that kills with lethal flatulence, to Beavis and Butthead sound effects.

- **Levels:** These are user-designed levels which can be used with the registered version of *Doom*, and some are obviously better than others. My thanks to all the *Doom* fans whose contributions I've enclosed!

- **Cheats:** These are simple hint files, tips, maps, and clues to where to find secret rooms, how to beat a level, etc.

Do we need to say that you better keep your original *Doom* backed up before you try to use any of these hacks?

Didn't think so.

DoomEd: The Real Thing

Who's It From? Geoff Allen

Where is It? X:\DOSHARE\DOOM-STUF

How Do I Use It? Unzip DMREAL.ZIP into a junk directory. Run SETUP in Windows. *DoomEd* must be specially configured to work on each computer.

What Do I Get? You get the registered *DoomEd: The Real Thing* editing program.

How Much? $15 to register, or $25 to register and get the source code.

How Do I Order? Geoff Allen, 7232 Kananasjis Dr. SW, Calgary, Alberta, Canada T2V 2N2.

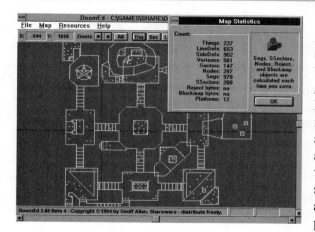

DoomEd: The Real Thing has a good Windows interface, using drop-down menus and icons. You can pull any element from *Doom*, alter it, and put it back. Music, sound effects, character images, and wall appearance can all be edited. You can also build a level from scratch, placing elevators, walls, hidden doors, sprites, powerups, and just about anything else anywhere you please.

Since *DoomEd*'s installation is a bit spotty, and the program should be loaded to the hard drive, we've included it in a *.ZIP file. Just unzip it to a junk directory, then run SETUP in Windows. If you do install it, make sure to keep track of the DOOMED.INI file in the Windows directory. The setup program will not understand it if you move *Doom* into another directory, and it must be edited manually.

Please Note! If you have to reinstall *DoomEd* or change the directory paths, you must delete DOOMED.INI in the WINDOWS directory.

Doom: DeHackEd

Who's It From? Dan Lottero

Where Is It? X:\DOSHARE\DOOM-STUF

How Do I Use It? Unzip DMHACK.ZIP into its own directory. Works from command line. See below.

What Do I Get? Version 1.3 of DeHackEd *Doom* editor, working with registered *Doom* 1.2.

How Do I Order? It seems like this is freeware, but please drop the author a line at dlottero@bu.edu to check on what he's doing and give any feedback.

DeHackEd is a DOS-based *Doom* editor, working with registered version 1.2, that allows you to change "thing tables" in DOOM.EXE file. As its author, Dan Lottero, points out, "Make fireballs invisible! Make missiles do 2000 points of damage! Make demons float!" Edit the "ammo tables," the "frame tables," create new looking items, or extra-fast shooting weapons! Two patch files, one for super-rapid-fire weapons, the other for morphing monsters, are also included. (Patch files save all info on frames, ammo, and things, not just changed data.) Check out DHEFUN02.TXT for more on how to change *Doom*.

DeHackEd works from the command line as follows:

```
dehacked <doomexe> -load <patchname> -save <patchname>
```

- **<doomexe>** is optional, and specifies a different location of the doom.exe file other than the current directory.

- **load <patchname>** will update the doom.exe file with the patch called <patchname>.

- **save <patchname>** will save the current doom.exe status to a patch file named <patchname>.

Sample Command Line:

```
dehacked c:\doom\doom.exe -load morfmons.deh
```

DoomCAD

Who's It From? Matt Tagliaferri

Where Is It? X:\DOSHARE\DOOM-STUF

How Do I Use It? Unzip DOOM-CAD.ZIP into its own directory.

What Do I Get? One cool editor.

How Much? $15

How Do I Order? Matt Tagliaferri, 4416 Brooklyn Ave., Cleveland, OH 44109.

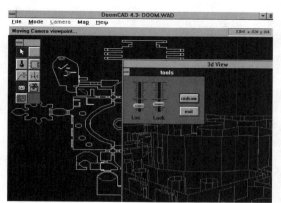

DoomCAD is my personal favorite among *Doom* editors. It features a clean, powerful Windows interface and a gaggle of features, all excellently implemented. The drop-down menus and icon palette make accessing various functions and switching between modes a snap. *DoomCAD* uses various colors to designate and edit creatures, objects, walls, and sectors, and includes a "Prefab" function to make placing objects like stairs and teleporters much easier. Plus, there's also a 3D viewer that allows you to see a line-rendered version of your level. *DoomCAD* has no sound, music, or sprite editing capabilities, but it's one powerful level editor.

DOOM LEVELS, HACKS, AND HINTS

So many *Doom* enhancements are popping up on bulletin board systems all over the country that it's impossible to keep up. New levels, goofy patches, maps, and other gewgaws give you valuable *Doom* help or simply make silly alterations to the game. Here's what we're giving you on this enclosed CD-ROM, all of them zipped and in the X:\DOSHARE\DOOMSTUF directory.

- **New Levels! (X:\DOSHARE\DOOMSTUF\DOOMWADS):** You wanted 'em, we got 'em: over *four dozen* gamer-designed levels uploaded to bulletin boards. They're located in one large directory called X:\DOSHARE\ DOOMSTUF\DOOMWADS. Just move the levels you want to use into your *Doom* directory. To work these levels either look for a *.BAT file with the same name, or type DOOM -FILE <levelname>.WAD. We've done all

ID SOFTWARE: DOOMED TO SUCCEED

By the rough estimate of Jay Wilbur, Business Manager of id Software, *Doom* Episode 1 is installed on somewhere between five and seven million computers. Ultimately, it will be the most installed game of all time, eclipsing *Wolfenstein*, the previous holder of that honor. Think about this for a second. A best-selling game from a major company can usually hope for a couple hundred thousand sales. A record-breaker like *The 7th Guest* stuns the industry with one million sales. But with shareware, the id folks get their product into the hands of literally millions of users, approximately one to two percent of whom buy the full game. This is for a product which has never been on retail shelves and has a negligible, at best, marketing budget.

That's not the kind of success larger companies can ignore.

The core group of id—John Carmack, Adrian Carmack (no relation), and John Romero—began hacking on games in their off time while working at game innovator Soft Disk. The first project was *Commander Keen*, a successful shareware game which led to *Wolfenstein*, an even bigger success, which, of course, led to *Doom*. They relocated to Madison, Wisconsin and then to Garland, Texas, with Kevin Cloud and Wilbur joining in the latter part of *Wolfenstein*. Their staff eventually expanded to ten: smaller than some companies' marketing department. At no point did they work with one of the big gaming companies, and their only truck with what might qualify as "mainstream" gaming would be their relations with shareware distributor Apogee and now CT Interactive. Did they ever think of working with a large company in order to bankroll their work? "It's not for us," Wilbur admits. "If there wasn't a big guy paying the payroll, some of the smaller companies may never have gotten started. We found a way to bootstrap it and we really didn't have to answer to anybody. Now we really like that. We don't want to have people say to us, 'You can't have that upside down cross or demon symbol in here.' Yeah, get outta here. We do what we want."

The key to id's success is simple, says Wilbur: "We write the games that we want to play. You'll find no bigger *Doom* fans than those of us here at id. (As a matter of fact, you may have heard of corporations having to ban *Doom*. I can confirm it: id software has had to ban *Doom*.) We don't go out there and say, 'Where's the niche in the marketplace?' and ask all the usual questions the suits-and-ties ask. We say, 'What's cool? What do we want to play?' We answer to no one. Sandy Petersson, who joined us from MicroProse, was used to working in big game companies with gobs of red tape. He noted that a game like *Doom* would likely never be developed in a major game company because of all the issues and all the red tape involved: the violence issue, the politically correct issues, the fact that you're shooting demons and demons reside in hell which is designed by Satan's interior decorator or whatever. It would just never go. We just sit down and say, 'Is this cool? It's cool. Let's do it.'"

The process usually begins with John Carmack, id's chief technical guru, sitting down and creating a new game engine: the next leap in id's technological achievements. Then they all sit around and, as Wilbur puts it, "make a really kicking game out of it." Right now, with a best seller and the lowest rate of return in the entire industry, id has quite a few venture capitalists and investment bankers knocking on their door. One key to their success is the creation of a frenzy of demand via street-level word-of-mouth. The shareware product is everywhere and everyone has heard about it. They follow that up with a retail version, in this case *Doom II*. "The sales of the retail product goes through the roof," Wilbur observes, "because there's a demand now. *Doom* Episode 1 is our *Mortal Kombat* or *Street Fighter* arcade machine: it's out there, there's a demand, and it builds to a fever pitch. Then, when we release the home version to the retail shops, the people are pounding the doors down to get it. Although it does pay to have a better mousetrap, certainly figuring out a better way to get your mousetrap to market is key. That's what we did. If you put something out there truly inspiring and truly top of the heap, the public will become your sales force."

we could to make sure these were good, working levels, but be warned: since different editors were used in many of these, they may simply lock at times. If you find one that locks regularly, please drop me a note.

- **Level Maps (DOOMSTUF\DOOMMAPS):** GIF images of level maps, marked with secret rooms, and other useful hints. Use a standard GIF viewer to look at them.

- **The "Barney" Patch (BARN3D.ZIP):** That's right: everyone's favorite purple dinosaur is inserted into *Doom*. Hear him sing "I looove youuuuu, you loooove meeee," while slinging fireballs at your head! See him explode into spurts of gore! A very sick and very funny patch. I passed this one along to my editor at *PC Gamer*, who was in the process of blowing the little purple bastard to bits when his young daughter walked in and, seeing "Barney dead," freaked out. So, make sure children aren't in the room! Unzip it into the *Doom* directory and type BARNEYGO.

- **The "Bunny" Patch (BUNNY3D.ZIP):** He keeps going, and going, and going...until you shotgun him into a pile of bunny fur. Changes Former Sergeants into a drum-beating bunny that packs a lethal blast. Good graphics and, when firing a rocket launcher, a sound effect saying, "He keeps going...." Unzip it into the *Doom* directory and type BUNNY3D to install and UNBUN-NY to de-install.

- **The "Dave" Patch (DAVEDM.ZIP):** This was weird enough to merit inclusion: David Letterman's smiling face looms large in the sky as you play *Doom*? Why? Beats me, but here it is. Unzip it into the *Doom* directory and type DAVEY to install.

- **The "Dalek" Patch (DALEK3D.ZIP):** Long to battle the Daleks from Dr. Who while playing *Doom*? Look no further: just unzip the file in the *Doom* directory and type DALEK3D to install.

- **The "Buttman" Patch (BUTTMAN.ZIP):** Turns Imps into an odd-looking monster which shoots balls of lethal flatulence. Hey, I don't make 'em, folks, I just pass 'em along. Unzip file into the *Doom* directory and type BUTTIN.

- **The "Beavis and Butthead" Patch (B_BDOOM.ZIP):** Replaces standard *Doom* sound effects with vintage Beavis and Butthead-type noises. Unzip into the *Doom* directory and type SOUND.

- **The "Aliens" Patch (DMALIEN\ALIENS.ZIP):** Replaces standard *Doom* sound effects and creatures with those from *Aliens*, including facehuggers and several different aliens. Type ALIENMNU to run.

- **RanDOOM (RDOOM165.ZIP):** Randomizes the placement of monsters and objects throughout the levels.

Terminator: Rampage

Who's It From? Bethesda Softworks	**What Do I Get?** Interactive demo
Where Is It? X:\DOSDEMO\RAMPAGE	**How Much?** N/A
	How Do I Order? Bethesda Softworks, 1370 Picard Dr., Rockville, MD 20850.
How Do I Use It? Type TERM at DOS prompt.	

The now-familiar first-person, ersatz-*Wolfenstein/Doom* action game is becoming so prominent that it seems like every other product is declaring itself a "*Doom-Killer*." Well, if you really like this type of game, then that's good news ...mostly. It's getting harder and harder to tell which games are worthwhile and which aren't.

If you're a fan of Arnold's *Terminator* movies (hey, who isn't?), then the decision is a little easier. *Terminator: Rampage* is the third in a series of *Terminator*-based games from Bethesda Softworks, and the one that has the best gameplay. As in the films, a handful of humans, led by John Conner, wage their ongoing battle to destroy the robotic SKYNET which has taken over their world. They now have a new weapon in this war: a forgotten suit of powered armor, giving the wearer unique strength and targeting abilities. It's your duty as a soldier to don the suit and make your way into SKYNET's nerve center to do them some damage.

Rampage plunges the gamer into the grim *Terminator* world, offering some chilling settings and thick atmosphere. Some of the familiar monsters from the movies are here, but an entire bestiary of robotic warriors has been added as well, making for a consistent freshness in opponents. And not all these monsters stay down when they go down. If you haven't killed them enough they may well get back up and attack you, probably from behind! There seem to be countless weapons to collect throughout the various levels, and each has a unique look and fire animation. To make things more challenging, there isn't a lot of ammo to be found, so you can't just unleash an unending barrage of firepower: you have to pick and choose when, how, and what to shoot, and conserve ammo.

While the graphics throughout *Rampage* are beautifully rendered, they don't process very well on lower speed machines, and even 486/50s seem to produce choppy results. The images are also oddly flat, undermining the illusion of three dimensions. Still, there's a lot of action and atmosphere, and a few unique twists, to keep *Rampage* interesting.

Corridor 7: Alien Invasion

Who's It From? Capstone, using id Software technology

Where Is It? X:\DOSDEMO\CORR7

How Do I Use It? Type CORR7 at DOS prompt.

What Do I Get? DOS demo, with one entire playable level.

How Much? $59.95

How Do I Order? IntraCorp. Inc., Airport Corporate Center, 7200 Corporate Center Dr., Ste. 500, Miami, FL 33126. (800) 468-7226.

Capstone's *Corridor 7: Alien Invasion* is slightly behind the curve on the technology front (it's no *Doom* or *CyClones*), but it's still a fun 3D action game with some atmospheric graphics and a good mix of weapons and monsters. Developed using id's *Wolfenstein 3D* engine, *Corridor 7* is a straightforward blast-'em-back-to-the-hell-they-came-from action game. The story is as simple as they come: you're sent into a top-secret underground military facility that is being overrun by monsters from beyond the beyond. It seems that an orb brought back from Mars is actually a trap set by aliens thousands of years earlier to alert them to the presence of other races. The aliens stream through a gateway opened by the orb,

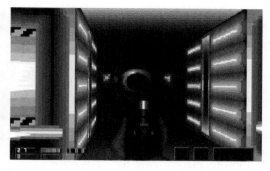

quickly take over the facility, and begin creating a force-field around the base. Once they have a firm foothold, they can conquer the planet at their leisure. A Special Forces Marine, you are told to enter the base, proceed to the 30th floor, go to Corridor 7 (where the orb is located), and assess the situation. In the course of your blood-letting, you pick up some of the base's advanced military technology—as well as alien weapons—to help with your battle. Of course, your communications are soon cut off, and you have to fight your way to Corridor 7 on your own and thwart the aliens' plans.

Though initially released as a disk-based game, *C7* is now available as an enhanced CD-ROM. Not only do you get 46 levels of action (instead of 30), more aliens, more weapons, CD-quality music, and new cinematics to further the story (story? what's that?), but the CD version also comes with modem and network play. Such features as a game randomizer, multiple difficulty levels, the ability to set mines on the levels, and a choice of either cooperative or "Deathmatch"-type games in head-to-head play mean there's enough here to satisfy action hounds. A couple of the monsters may be somewhat silly looking (it's hard to take a monster seriously when it's the same shade of purple as Barney the Dinosaur), but overall there's plenty here to keep you rolling right along.

Use the arrow keys to steer, CTRL to fire, Spacebar to open doors, TAB to see the map, and M to drop a mine.

Blake Stone

Who's It From? Apogee

Where Is It? X:\DOSHARE\BSTONE

How Do I Use It? Type BSTONE at DOS prompt.

What Do I Get? First set of levels.

What Am I Missing? Five more sets of levels, introduction, cheat keys, hint book, and registered copy.

How Much? $59.95

How Do I Order? Apogee, 3960 Broadway, Suite 235, Garland, TX 75043. (800) APOGEE1.

Blake Stone was probably the earliest of the *Wolfenstein 3D* clones, and it still holds up pretty well despite being technologically upstaged by other shooters. Though a lot of people didn't quite care for this when it came out, on the whole they tended to be hardcore *Wolfenstein 3D*ers: judged on its own, *Blake Stone* is just good-ole, fast-moving fun. No brilliant graphics or sound, but lotsa stuff to shoot.

It's some time in the future, and Blake Stone, one of the British government's best secret operatives, is being sent to planet Solan to infiltrate the STAR institute. No one quite knows what's going on there, but it seems the mad geneticist (you can never have enough mad geneticists for this kind of game) Dr. Goldfire has...well, something evil planned for the universe and, of course, Blake is the only man who can etc, etc. You have to fight your way through each level of the institute, killing monsters and collecting the red access keys to get to the next level. Food, medkits, ammo, new weapons, and the usual array of useful stuff are all on hand to help you along.

Blake doesn't have as keen a sense of humor as *W3D*, but it makes up for it with some interesting monsters and tricks. For instance, each level has a number of informants who look like scientists. Get close to them and click the space bar, and they'll give you a small tip about the level. Some of these are more useful that others, but as a general policy don't kill informants. Health is also handled in a more interesting way than in *W3D*. Some people (read: dead people) carry food tokens that you can pick up. Stick these into any food machine (just walk up to the machine and click the Spacebar), and you get some food to increase your health levels a bit.

CyClones

Who's It From? Created by Raven, released by SSI.

Where Is It? X:\DOSDEMO\CYCLONES

How Do I Use It? Type CYCLONES at DOS prompt. Please note: this demo is very unforgiving to any computer under a 486SX.

What Do I Get? One playable level-in-progress.

How Much? $55.00

How Do I Order? SSI, 675 Almanor Ave., Ste. 201, Sunnyvale, CA 94086-2901. (800) 245-4525.

id's success has not been lost on the rest of the industry. There is definitely a demand for *Doom*-type first person shooters, and a new batch are making their way to the marketplace. At the forefront of this push are those who are working with id directly by licensing the *Doom* engine and adapting it for their own needs, one of the best being SSI's *CyClones*, developed by Raven Software. Raven is no newcomer to first person gaming (see sidebar): their *Shadowcaster* game, distributed by Origin, uses a greatly enhanced id engine to create a terrific role-playing fantasy game involving magic and morphing. (Do yourself a favor and check out the CD-ROM version.) They also recently completed *Heretic*, which is available as shareware from id. *CyClones* takes this technology into a whole new area, modifying the in-your-face feel of *Doom* to include inventory items, more delicate controls, and some really hot new features.

In *CyClones*, some nasty aliens are coming to earth and taking tissue samples in order to create an army of cybernetic, partly human soldiers called CyClones. These CyClones are almost ready, and it's your job to thwart the aliens' schemes. As a member of a secret military program, you've been equipped with cutting-edge weaponry and armor. Sent to penetrate the main alien compound, you have to take out as many as you can while learning just how far they've gotten. This first level of *CyClones* will give you a pretty good taste of what awaits

---

CyClones **Tips**

- **Search each alien body for useful things. You'll find ammo, keys, and other things essential to your survival.**

- **Proceed slowly and use your Gauss gun with some discretion: at least in this version, there aren't as many ammo packs as there are in *Doom*.**

- **Search for hidden doors by running your icon over walls. If it turns purple, there's a door there. One hides the chaingun.**

- **After the game begins, and you've killed that first alien up ahead, search the nearest building on the right. There's a medkit there to restore your health. Keep it in inventory, and when you need it, click on it.**

RAVEN: HIRED GUNS

The hardest decision small gaming companies face is how to develop their product and get it to market. Do they find sources of capital from outside the gaming industry, then attempt to distribute it themselves? Do they let someone else handle distribution? Do they try to get one of the big companies to pick up their product and fund its completion? Each path has its pros and cons, and one company that has seen it all is Raven Software, of Madison, Wisconsin. One of many independents who work with large publishers to get their products financed and to market, Raven is also experimenting with shareware distribution and other channels, trying all possible ways and seeing which is best at getting the product to the most people, and which produces the most revenue.

Raven's first big PC splash was *Shadowcaster*, a neat twist on first-person role-playing games in which the player could morph into a number of different creatures. Funded and released by Origin Systems and featuring technology from id, *Shadowcaster* (featured in the role-playing section) showed that the programmers at Raven know how to make good games. Following *Shadowcaster* with the slick *CyClones* (released by SSI, see entry above), an as yet untitled game for Origin, and *Heretic*, a shareware title released by id, means the guys at Raven are having a mighty busy year.

Victor Penman, Raven's VP of Product Development, has worked for several large companies, such as Electronic Arts, and is familiar with how they work: "Sometimes you have to go through a lot of different approval processes. Working on the outside there are less approval processes, but sometimes you send stuff off to a publisher, it comes back, and you're told to change it, sometimes without ever really being told why. I can think of a couple instances in the past where changes came up that appeared to be somewhat arbitrary. That can be frustrating. I think that right now we have a really good relationship with everyone we're working with."

With a flurry of new projects all going simultaneously, Raven has gone from four to twenty employees in little over a year. Working with different companies means they have a rare opportunity to compare how different kinds of distribution really work, and, as VP Brian Raffel observes, "The fact that we're putting out all these games in all these different ways will show us where we'll ultimately go. We're kind of testing the waters and finding out which way we want to go."

Penman agrees: "I think the independent publishers are finding that a fairly small number of large publishers have the distribution locked up, and there's not a lot of leeway. I would say that the standard royalty deal with the big publisher would be about 15% of what the publisher gets, while the royalty deal with shareware is much better. On a per-unit basis, you're better with shareware, but you don't reach as big a market that way. We're about to publish our first shareware product, so we don't know what will happen yet, but I expect we would make more money from shareware, with much smaller distribution and net sales, than with normal retail channels. There are reasons for that: the retailer takes some, the publisher takes some, the distributors take some, and ultimately you get a fairly small percentage of what the publisher gets."

It's pretty much a win/win situation for publishers who go out of house for their development. The commitment isn't as deep or expensive, and they can cut an outside developer loose much easier than they can an employee. The fact that there are large creative wells to be mined outside of the mainstream is one incentive, but the bottom line for hiring outside developers is often financial. "The big companies have a lot of overhead," Penman observes, "and that shows up on their costs to do a product internally. Also, from a financial standpoint, when someone gives us an advance to do a product,

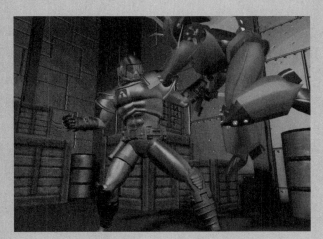

A cut scene from Raven's *CyClones*.

we sort of owe that money back. So, on their books, they're not actually out that money, whereas if they do the project internally, it shows up as an expense and it lowers their profitability. My own opinion is that most of the push for doing work on the outside is a financial push. That's not to say that finding really creative people on the outside is not a good thing that publishers like to do, because they go after that very aggressively. But the economics of doing games inside can be pretty tough sometimes."

you. It features a series of warehouses that form a maze-like complex. The best way to control the game is to use the keypad for movement and the mouse for aiming. This may be tricky at first, but you'll soon get used to it. Unlike *Doom*, the gun in *CyClones* tracks with the movement of your mouse, allowing you to aim anywhere on the screen. The icon color is important to understanding the operation of *CyClones*: if the icon is orange, it's over an enemy unit; if it's green, it means that an item may be used or put into inventory; if it's purple, then it's over a door. There are secret doors, and one hides a chaingun, so watch that icon color. To shoot at something, place the icon over it and click the left mouse button; to open a door or select something on screen, click right. Clicking on the automap function allows you to see a zoomable, 3D view of the landscape from above. In the map view, you can use the mouse to redirect the flashlight beam anywhere, with a little window in the upper left-hand corner showing just what the light reveals.

Halloween Harry

Who's It From? Sub Zero Software, Binary Illusions, and Apogee

Where Is It? X:\DOSHARE\HHARRY

How Do I Use It? Type HH1 at the DOS prompt

What Do I Get? One whole level of action.

What Am I Missing? Three more levels.

How Much? $29.95

How Do I Order? Apogee, 3960 Broadway, Suite 235, Garland, TX 75043. (800) APOGEE1.

Well, it's happened *yet again*! Aliens have come to earth, parked a huge spaceship under Wall Street, and started collecting earthlings in order to turn them into flesh-eating zombies so they can use them as slave labor unless, of course, the Earth capitulates now and bows down before the Great—yet Evil—alien lord.

Don't you just hate when that happens? Sorta like being trapped in an Ed Wood movie with Arnold Schwarzenegger.

Of course Harry is the only person who can save the day. Armed with a flame thrower, some rockets, a jet pack, and the intermittent ability to communicate with his able contact on the outside, Harry must get from level to level, release hostages, kill zombies, pick up new weapons, etc. This is an amiably silly little side-scrolling Mario-esque game, with some cute graphics and even a few challenges.

Raptor

Who's It From? Developed by Cygnus Studio, distributed by Apogee

Where Is It? X:\DOSHARE\RAPTOR

How Do I Use It? Copy to hard drive and type SETUP to configure.

What Do I Get? First sector of the shareware game.

What am I Missing? Two additional, and more difficult, sectors.

How Much? $34.95

How Do I Order? Apogee, 3960 Broadway, Suite 235, Garland, TX 75043. (800) APOGEE1.

The first-person shooter may be the most popular type of action game right now, but the space arcade game is a close second. Taken from a variety of perspectives—mostly top-down views, but also cockpit simulators and side-scrolling games—the space arcade game is almost its own category. The point of these games is even more simple than

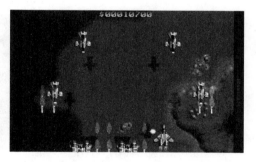

first person shooters: navigate a spaceship through various landscapes and blast other spaceships, asteroids, or buildings. One of the best recent examples of this sub-genre is undoubtedly *Raptor*.

Next to *Doom*, *Raptor* may be one of the hottest things to hit shareware in a long, long time. There is nothing particularly earth-shattering about its gameplay or design: it doesn't do anything much new, it just does it all exceedingly well. Like Origin's *Privateer*, *Raptor* gives you a ship and makes you a hired gun: a mercenary who'll take on any ship-killing job as long as there's a paycheck in it. Your space ship is placed at the bottom of a continuous, vertically scrolling landscape filled with enemy threats and buildings. Using a joystick, a mouse, or arrow keys, you can steer the ship anywhere on the screen and fire at the onrushing targets. Some ships fly in tight patterns, zipping quickly above the terrain and firing straight ahead, while others move slowly from top to bottom, shooting from their sides. On the ground, bridges, carriers, gun emplacements, storage tubes, and numerous buildings all provide multiple targets, and all should be blasted to bits. All of this leads, in most cases, to final confrontations with large, ponderously slow but heavily armed and armored "motherships."

Depending on what difficulty level you choose, you have a certain amount of power available for shields. This power will be steadily whittled away by hits, until you explode in a most impressive fireball. Enough shielding must be left for the final confrontation on each level, since the mother ship fires numerous guns simultaneously and most hit their target: you. Each target you destroy adds more money to your coffers, allowing you to buy ship enhancements to go kill more ships, and so on. There are some handsome narrative sequences and a good inter-face, but the game graphics themselves are the real standout. *Raptor* is gorgeous: simply one of the best-looking scrolling-shooters ever. The scrolling seems a bit slow in the beginning, but that slowness doesn't seem to make the game any less challenging, and you have more time to admire that lovely scenery.

Zone 66

Who's It From? Created by Renaissance Productions, distributed by Epic MegaGames

Where Is It? X:\DOSHARE\ZONE66

How Do I Use It? Type ZONE66 at the DOS prompt. (You need to run with a "clean" configuration, so either make a boot disk (see Introduction) or, with DOS 6.0 or later, hit F5 on bootup.

What Do I Get? First episode: "Foreign Shores."

What Am I Missing? Three more episodes, plus an optional add-on pack of four episodes, bringing the total to eight.

How Much? For a registered copy featuring the first four episodes and cheat keys, send $30 (for the game plus the add-on pack, send $45).

How Do I Order? Epic MegaGames, 354 NE Greenwood Ave., Ste. 108, Bend, OR 97701-4631. (800) 972-7434.

If you can get this one running, and they sure didn't make it easy, you'll find a top-down flying/shooting game with a solid story and some peachy graphics. Featuring Japanimation-style cut scenes, *Zone 66* puts you in the role of an ex-pilot with the Global Security Agency: the military wing of the planetary government. Terrorists are a constant threat, and now they've gotten hold of a few old-style nuclear warheads, which they're detonating in major cities. When your wife and child are killed in one of the blasts, you are determined to fight the terrorists again, and once more take to the air to strike at enemy targets.

Zone 66 is not an easy game to play, since the top-down perspective doesn't let you see just what direction ongoing air threats are attacking from. Fighting air-to-air is quite difficult to master, but once you do you'll find this a fast-paced yet strategically challenging game. The arrow in the lower right-hand corner shows the direction you need to head for one of two locations. If you hit "T," the arrow points to the main bombing targets. If you hit "B," it points to the nearest landing pad for refueling and repairs. On the map at the top of the screen white dots are prime targets, and blue dots are landing pads. Two modes help you with evasions: shadow mode (hit the C key until the S icon comes up) makes you briefly invisible, while evasion mode (hit the C key until the E icon comes up), gives you a burst of speed.

The point of most missions is to destroy ground targets, and there are a healthy selection of bombs, from firebombs to "megabombs," to help with the task. Bombing major targets while fending off wave after wave of air assault and lethal ground fire isn't easy! But with some practice, you'll find yourself totally engrossed with this rather complex title.

☆ X-Wing ☆

Who's It From? LucasArts

Where Is It? X:\DOSDEMO\XWING

How Do I Use It? See special instructions.

What Do I Get? Non-Interactive demo.

How Much? $69.95

How Do I Order? LucasArts Games, P.O. Box 10307, San Rafael, CA 94912. (800) STAR WARS.

For many years, there was really only one high-end, brand name commercial space combat game to have, and that was *Wing Commander*. Featuring a storyline punctuated by combat sequences, *Wing Commander* was a true landmark in computer gaming, and continues to this day to be one of the finest of this genre as Origin Systems continues to push it ever-further for a new generation of gamers.

But then LucasArts announced that it was going to give *Wing Commander* a run for its money: they were actually going to put gamers *inside* some of the most popular movies of all time: the *Star Wars* trilogy. You would actually fly for the

rebels, side-by-side with Luke Skywalker, fighting Darth Vader's TIE Fighters and the evil Empire.

X-Wing proved to be everything it promised to be and more. It delivered familiar characters, settings, storylines, and ships in a game that was so much fun that fans couldn't get enough. Built around a new, stylish engine and featuring narrative cut scenes, terrific sounds, and high-end graphics, it truly offers something new. X-Wings, Y-Wings, A-Wings, and, in an add-on disk, B-Wings, are all available for missions. Players are able to gain proficiency with the various ships in ever-more-difficult proving ground scenarios, fly single historical missions, or join several long campaigns against the Empire. From fiery dogfights with TIE fighters, to bombing runs, to the final "trench run" to destroy the Death Star (taken right from the movie), you experience an entire range of combat action. The story-line was continued in two add-on disks: *Imperial Pursuit* and *B-Wing*.

Now, it's all available on a single CD-ROM, with the addition of full speech support (including the voices of some actors from the films), enhanced graphics with Gouraud shading, new missions, and enhanced animations. Playable from the CD-ROM, it is yet another must-have addition to any gamer's library, and it paves the way for one of the most exciting new titles of the year: its sequel, *TIE Fighter*.

X-Wing Special Instructions

When you're in the XWING subdirectory, use the following commands to run the demo for your particular sound board:

- Type XBLAST if you have a Soundblaster.
- Type XADLIB if you have an Ad-Lib Board.
- Type XLOWEND for slower machines with no sound.

☆ TIE Fighter ☆

Who's It From? LucasArts	**What Do I Get?** Interactive demo.
Where Is It? X:\DOSDEMO\TIE	**How Much?** $69.95
How Do I Use It? Type TIEDEMO at DOS prompt.	**How Do I Order?** LucasArts Games, P.O. Box 10307, San Rafael, CA 94912. (800) STAR WARS.

There's no two ways about it: *TIE Fighter* smokes. I haven't seen a space flight simulator this good since...well, since LucasArts released *X-Wing*, *TIE Fighter*'s much-honored predecessor (see previous entry). Drawing on George Lucas's *Star Wars* universe, which over the years has become ingrained in the American psyche, these flight sims put you not only in

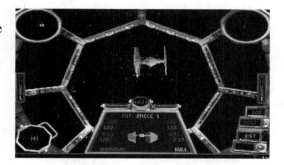

the cockpit of a rebel X-Wing fighter or Empire TIE Fighter, but also inside a story as good and evil battle for control of the galaxy. Deftly weaving storylines throughout burning action sequences, they raise the stakes in the realm of space-flight sims.

X-Wing made you a rebel pilot, allowing you to fly X-Wings, B-Wings, Y-Wings, and A-Wings against the Emperor. The missions—over fifty in the initial release, plus add-on disks—ranged from escorts to strikes to intense dogfighting to a final shoot out in the trenches of the Death Star itself, recreating the final scene from *Star Wars*. Now, in *TIE Fighter*, it's time to fight from the other side, and, for various reasons, it's even better this time around. Why, you may ask. Well, a year has passed and technology—graphics, sound effects and music—are even better this time around. Certain elements—the training

TIE-Fighter Control Tips

You can actually fly the demo that's included, but be aware that the final version looks, sounds, and controls *much* better. Joystick response is smoother, and the sound effects are much better executed than the flimsy laser blasts in the demo. Still, it'll give you an idea of what you'll be facing. Use Enter to fire, steer with a joystick or the keyboard, and hit "G" to change the gun configuration.

THE SHIPS OF *TIE FIGHTER*

In *TIE Fighter,* you can train and fly missions in five different ships, each with its own unique qualities and abilities. Each ship has varying amounts of guns, missiles, shields and armor, and speed. Guns, for example, come in two types:

- *ion cannons* run off the engine, draining power faster and making for a weaker weapon
- *laser cannons* run off a separate power source, and are therefore more powerful and don't put as much stress on the engine

Some ships fire concussion missiles or even "dumb" (unguided) bombs. Each has armor (the higher the RU rating, the better), and some have electronic shields.

TIE Starfighter
Cannons: two laser cannons
Missiles: none
Shields: none/15RU
Speed: 100

TIE Interceptor
Cannons: two laser cannons
Missiles: none
Shields: none/20 RU
Speed: 110

Assault Gunboat
Cannons: two laser cannons & two ion cannons
Missiles: 16 concussion
Shields: 100SBD/50RU
Speed: 90

TIE Advanced
Cannons: four laser cannons
Missiles: two general purpose launchers
Shields: 100SBD/20RU
Speed: 145

TIE Bomber
Cannons: two laser cannons
Missiles: 6 concussion missiles OR 4 torpedoes
Shields: none/50RU
Speed: 80

mode, cut scenes, an intriguing subplot—all add greatly to the entire experience. Plus, there are the TIE craft themselves: the TIE Fighter, TIE Bomber, TIE Interceptor, TIE Advanced, Assault Gunboat, and the new XG-1 Star Wing. If you played *X-Wing*, you'll recall how fast and nimble these things were as opponents. Well, now *you're* flying them, and they really *move*. And finally, *TIE Fighter* is probably better than its predecessor because, let's admit it: the villain is always more interesting than the hero. Face it, Luke Skywalker was a dork, but Darth Vader? He dresses like a member of KISS, has mysterious powers, and scares the crap out of everyone. Plus, Stormtroopers got to wear that really cherry body armor. The Dark Side of the Force was always a bit more interesting, and now it's your turn to fight for it.

TIE Fighter has numerous choices for play, but the best place to start is with training missions to sharpen your skills. The first ones aren't nearly as deadly-dull as the first *X-Wing* training missions, which seemed interminable. They get you right into the action and include in-mission directions to help you learn the ropes. Once you beat all these and test the different TIEs, you can start working on the storyline, or just do some one-shot missions to brush up. You create a pilot identity and carry it through the story—unless he gets scorched—rising through the ranks of the Imperial Navy and earning medals (if you're worthy). Woven throughout the missions is the story of the Empire's fight against the "rebel terrorists" and a subplot dealing with a secret society of Empire pilots who make you an offer.

If you want space combat, look no further: this is simply the best space simulator ever. Sound like hyperbole? Fly it for yourself and see.

Solar Winds

Who's It From? Developed by Stone Interactive Media, distributed by Epic MegaGames

Where Is It? X:\DOSHARE\SOLAR

How Do I Use It? Type SOLAR1 at DOS prompt.

What Do I Get? Episode 1

What Am I Missing? Registered version of Episode 1, Episode 2, hint book, cheat codes, and a disk full of other Epic shareware.

How Much? $30

How Do I Order? Epic MegaGames, 354 NE Greenwood Ave., Ste. 108, Bend, OR 97701-4631. (800) 972-7434.

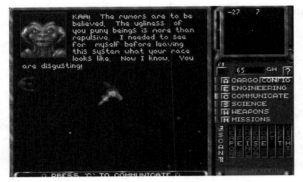

While not an altogether successful game, *Solar Winds* is certainly an interesting one with some standout elements. More than just a top-down space-shooter, *Solar Winds* uses a detailed story, character interaction, and various ship systems functions to create a narrative space game punctuated by arcade sequences.

It's far in the future (isn't it always?), and human earthlings are on the verge of coming into contact with other humans—distant ancestors of the earthlings—in another galaxy. As Jake Stone, a pilot-for-hire, you're approached by a man named Kane as the game opens. Kane offers you a job: go to a certain sector, capture an enemy of the state, and return him for a reward. When you finally catch up to this enemy, he claims he's a scientist who has valuable information and is being hunted by the government, who want to keep that information secret. It turns out that he is on the verge of creating technology that will allow people to travel to other galaxies: something which the government, for their own reasons, don't want to happen. He begs you to join his side and help him, and at that point you have to decide who you can trust: the scientist or Kane.

Solar Winds is designed around a central screen showing one small sector at a time, with your space craft centered in the middle. Ship functions, such as weapons, shields, storage, communications, and power, are controlled by a series of simple menus to the right of the screen. Each time you accept a mission, you are given sector coordinates, and you simply point the ship in the direction of the sector and press the up arrow for acceleration. Once at the location, you can make contact with whomever is there and complete your mission, much like Origin's *Privateer*. Unfortunately, navigation from one sector to another is not particularly fast, so the game tends to drag at points while you wait to arrive at your destination. And, if you're looking for a fast-paced arcade game, this isn't it; combat is sporadic, at least in the beginning. The emphasis here is on story and character, and on these fronts it succeeds, making for a somewhat unconventional space action game.

Quatra Command

Who's It From? Playdoe Entertainment Software

Where Is It? X:\WINGAMES\ QUATRA

How Do I Use It? Run QUATRA in Windows.

What Do I Get? First three levels of shareware release.

What Am I Missing? Lots more levels!

How Much? $22

How Do I Order? Playdoe Entertainment Software, 2412 Desert Oak Dr., Palmdale, CA 93550.

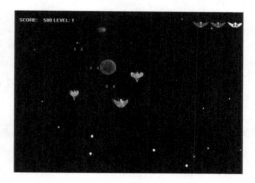

You will not believe how cool the graphics and sound in this Windows game are. A simple coin-op style space shooter, *Quatra*'s fast action and terrific visuals make it stand out. You're in control of a spaceship that can move up, down, left, and right with arrow keys, and shoot with the spacebar. Meteors both large and small, and all manner of spacecraft rocket at you from offscreen. Some of the alien spaceships are dumb and slow, others are tenacious and stick with you, while still others fire what seem to be guided rockets. The best Windows space shooter!

Stellar Warrior

Who's It From? Michael McAuliffe

Where Is It? X:\WINGAMES\STELLAR

How Do I Use It? Run the file SWR10.EXE in Windows.

What Do I Get? A small, multi-level space game.

What Am I Missing? Registration.

How Much? $10.00

How Do I Order? Michael McAuliffe, P.O. Box 3452, Reno, NV 89505. CIS: 70216,303.

Stellar Warrior is a little space arcade game for Windows, running inside a tiny window perfect for when the boss may be hovering nearby. Your goal is to stay alive as long as possible while shooting all of the other spacecraft. The arrow keys move your spaceship around the screen and the spacebar fires. If you are hit once or if too many ships sneak by, you'll be destroyed. Each level lasts a set amount of time, the higher levels lasting longer and the ships coming faster.

Jill of the Jungle

Who's It From? Epic MegaGames

Where Is It? X:\DOSHARE\JILL

How Do I Use It? Type JILL1 at the DOS prompt.

What Do I Get? Volume I, the first few levels of the game.

What Am I Missing? Lots more levels.

How Much? $30

How Do I Order? Epic MegaGames, 354 NE Greenwood Ave., Ste. 108, Bend, OR 97701-4631. (800) 972-7434.

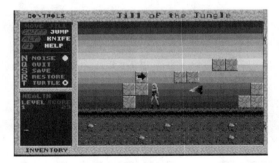

Jill of the Jungle is a side-scrolling, arcade adventure game that still holds up well after several years. Jill, our heroine, has to run, jump, and climb her way through a number of jungle adventures, picking up points and dodging death. Threats range from snakes, crocodiles (or are they alligators?), killer crabs, and other denizens of the jungle, to pungee sticks, fire, boulders, and all sorts of things designed to make Jill have a really bad hair day. Use the arrow keys to run and climb up or down, the space bar to open or close things, the SHIFT key to jump (watch those rolling boulders!), and the ALT key to throw one of the weapons you pick up along the way. Look for health bonuses, such as the floating apples, and keep on running.

Prairie Dog Hunts

Who's It From? Ian Firth/Diversions Software

Where Is It? X:\WINGAMES\WIN-DOG and X:\WINGAMES\WINDOG2

How Do I Use It? Prairie Dog Hunt: Run WINDOG from Windows. Prairie Dog Hunt 2: Run PDH2JD from Windows.

What Do I Get? Shootin' games.

What Am I Missing? Peace of mind.

How Much? PDH: $15; PDH2: $10

How Do I Order? Ian Firth, Diversions Software, 966 Kramer Court, Aurora, CO 80010. CIS: 76450,3711.

Another couple bits of fluff, but well-done and entertaining ones, at that. *Prairie Dog Hunt* and *Prarie Dog Hunt II: Judgement Day* feature quite nice graphics and silly sound effects, as you shoot prairie dogs popping up out of their holes. You have various weapons (different ones for each game), and get to set the amount of ammo you start with and the amount of prairie dogs you get to shoot.

To start either *Prairie Dog Hunt*, click on the little prairie dog with the crosshairs centered on him, then on the 'GO HUNTING' button. The game starts with a default prairie dog count of 20 and unlimited ammunition. You can change the dog amount to "A Bunch" (50 dogs) or "Dog Master" (100 dogs), and the ammo amount to "Limited Ammo" (10 for pellet gun, 6 for 44 Mag and 4 for shotgun) and "Dog Master" (6 for pellet gun, 4 for 44 Mag and 2 for shotgun). When you're ready to start hunting, just click on Prairie Dog Call and select a weapon. Fire by placing the icon over the dog and clicking the left mouse button. The pellet gun requires two hits to kill, the .44 magnum one, and the shot gun takes out all visible dogs. If they get too close, you'll get rabies.

Parents and animal rights people please note: These are violent games, with little dogs bitin' the dust in a splatter of blood, so don't let the kiddies play if you're easily bothered by this sort of thing. No actual prairie dogs were killed in the making of this game (though we did try).

GopherIt!

Who's It From? John Di Troia

Where Is It? X:\WINGAMES\ GOPHERIT

How Do I Use It? Run GOPHERIT.EXE in Windows.

What Do I Get? Lotsa gopher-whacking levels.

How Much? $5 to just register, $12 to get a copy on disk

How Do I Order? John Di Troia, 5 Mt Pleasant St., Saugus, MA 01906.

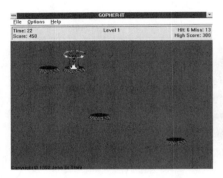

It's simple: stop the gophers from overrunning your lawn. This is accomplished by bopping them with an animal-safe padded club (it'll just stun 'em). Position the mouse cursor over the gopher (or other critter) and click the left mouse button. Points are awarded for each object hit, while 50 points are deducted for each miss. A hit-miss ratio of 50% is required to continue to the next level. New objects will appear and speeds will increase as successive levels are reached. A low rent "Whack-a-Mole." Kids seem to love it.

Adventures of MicroMan

Who's It From? Brian L. Goble

Where Is It? X:\WINGAMES\ MICROMAN

How Do I Use It? Run MICRO1.EXE in Windows.

What Do I Get? Adventure 1: Crazy Computers for 30 day trial.

What Am I Missing? Registered ver-

sion of Adventure 1, with cheat mode, maps, tips, and hints; Adventure 2: Savage Stones, plus a bonus Windows app, *WallMan*.

How Much? $25

How Do I Order? Brian L. Goble, 2218 Franklin Ave. E., Seattle, WA 98102. Internet: goble@u.washington.edu.

As MicroMan, you run, jump, duck, climb, and shoot your way past various enemies, while exploring new areas and collecting special powerups. MicroMan, once a normal-sized guy named Bob, was shrunk by the evil Dr. Schnapps' miniaturization machine, which subsequently exploded, trapping him at his wee-tiny size. Finding himself in a strange and hostile world, his only mission is to explore and stay alive.

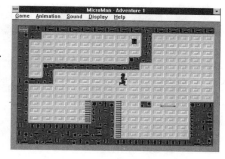

To play, select "New Game" from the "File" menu and begin. You use the arrow keys to move up, down, and side to side, the space-bar to jump (holding it down longer to jump higher), and the Insert key to shoot. Just keep moving to the right to explore new rooms.

Runner

Who's It From? SouthBay Software

Where Is It? X:\WINGAMES\ RUNNER

How Do I Use It? Run RUNNER.EXE from Windows.

What Do I Get? A few levels.

What Am I Missing? Registered version, the latest version, phone support, additional levels, and the endgame.

How Much? $19.95

How Do I Order? SouthBay Software, P.O. Box 871, Torrance, CA 90508. Phone/Fax: (310) 320-0614. CIS: 70564,3210.

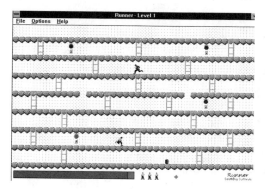

This is an unusual *Lode Runner* clone that seems almost to run in slow motion on my computer (a Pentium). Basically, you have the traditional sideview screen featuring ladders, jump offs, and numerous levels. As the story goes, you are trapped on a distant planet and out of fuel. You need to navigate through hazards, avoid being nabbed by the bad guy, and get enough fuel for your vehicle. The bad guy starts at the top, you at the bottom. By climbing ladders, you ascend levels, making sure to trigger all the traffic lights from red to green along the way. Of course, the bad guy is trying to get you as well, making this a bit tricky. Make sure to pick up the fuel thingies!

WinFight

Who's It From? Giovanni & Paolo Cignoni

Where Is It? X:\WINGAMES\WIN-FIGHT

How Do I Use It? Run WINFIGHT.EXE from Windows.

What Do I Get? Freeware shooter.

What Am I Missing? Nothing.

How Do I Order? Viale G. Amendola 39, 57025 Piombino LI, Italy. Giovanni Cignoni: cygnus@di.unipi.it; Paolo Cignoni: cignoni@suncube.cnuce.cnr.it.

WinFight is more SillyWare: a pop-up Windows shoot-out with a range of difficulty levels. To fight immediately, select Fight Now! from Game menu, or press the F2 key. A gunfighter will pop up, and you shoot by placing the cursor over him and clicking the left mouse button. Clicking the right button ends the fight. You can also set it for Timed Fight (which causes the gunfighter to pop up randomly while you're working), and adjust the difficulty level from Town Drunk to Wyatt Earp.

Bow and Arrow

Who's It From? John Di Troia

Where Is It? X:\WINGAMES\B&ARROW

How Do I Use It? Run B&ARROW.EXE from Windows.

What Do I Get? First few levels of shareware.

How Much? $5.00 to register, $12 to get extensive online help and hints, more levels (including a duel with the Black Archer), and sound support.

How Do I Order? John Di Troia, 5 Mt Pleasant St., Saugus, MA 01906.

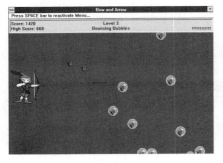

I found myself oddly hooked on this little archery game. *Bow and Arrow* seems so easy at first, but in fact it can be a bit tricky. You're given control of an archer, a certain number of arrows, and told to hit the moving targets. Easy, right?

Not always. Controlling it is not a problem, since it's all based around the mouse:

click right to load a new arrow, click and hold the left mouse button to draw the bowstring, and then release the left button to fire. Clicking left and dragging up or down allows you to reposition the archers.

The first set of targets, a row of balloons, takes a few tries to hit right. The problem lies in the fact that the balloons are floating upward at a steady speed, but each one is a different distance from you, so that the arc of fire changes with each balloon shot. You have to keep aiming higher to get the arrow to the right place on time. Of course, timing it so you can take out several balloons at once is preferred. Things get a bit more complex when other colored balloons are added. In the second set, you have to hit the red balloons while avoiding the yellow balloons, but they float upward at different speeds and in different directions. Then there's the butterflies-in-bubbles and, well...there are many more archery challenges to play with, and the registered versions add more yet.

Check it out. You might be pleasantly surprised.

MechWarrior 2: The Clans

Who's It From? Activision

Where Is It? X:\DOSDEMO\MECH2

How Do I Use It? Type MW2DEMO at DOS prompt.

What Do I Get? Interactive demo.

How Much? N/A

How Do I Order? Activision, 11601 Wilshire Blvd., 10th Floor, Los Angeles, CA 90025. (800) 477-3650.

Activision has been hard at work on this game for so long it's hard to even recall when we first started hearing about it. No promises, but *MechWarrior 2: The Clans* may be out by the time you read this. Or maybe not. Anyone who follows computer games knows that you can put about as much faith in release dates as in Michael Milken stock tips.

But, as they say, it will be worth the wait. Based on the *BattleTech* board games, a detailed world created by the FASA corporation, *MechWarrior 2* is a follow-up to the grandaddy of battling robot games. The premise puts you far in the future, with various noble house fighting for control of the "Inner Sphere." These battles are interrupted, however, by the return of The Clans— descendants of the MechWarriors who fled the Inner Sphere aeons ago—who have come to regain control. The technology of their battle-robots is far beyond that of the Houses, who decide to put aside their differences to attack the Clans.

As a young MechWarrior, you rise quickly through the ranks, controlling the two-legged battling mech robots in a series of missions to defeat the Clans. You play the game from the cockpit of a mech, controlling it as it roams the landscape to find and confront the enemy. Like an earth-bound flight sim, *MechWarrior 2* provides plenty of metal-grinding action and lots of 'bots to choose from. Plus, Activision plans to keep more coming with numerous add-on disks, head-to-head play, and lots of surprises.

Megatron

Who's It From? Stanley Design Group

Where Is It? X:\DOSHARE\MEGA-TRON

How Do I Use It? Type MEGA at DOS prompt.

What Do I Get? Two robots and various maps to play on.

How Much? $28.50

How Do I Order? John Dee Stanley, 6959 California Ave. SW, Seattle, WA 98136.

When you begin *Megatron*, you can elect to play one of two robots armed to the teeth and ready for action. The other can either be handled by a fairly capable computer AI, or by a friend using the modem option. You each begin in a different part of a series of mazes and are given the simple task of hunting down and killing the other. Your robots fire rockets and can also lay mines to slow the opponent's progress. *Megatron* comes with a variety of mazes and features pretty good graphics and sound. Playing it by yourself is okay, but playing head-to-head is the real delight, since that other robot is probably a friend, and there's nothing quite like stalking a friend through a maze with an armed robot.

Spectre VR

Who's It From? Velocity

Where Is It? X:\DOSDEMO\SPECTRE

How Do I Use It? Type DEMO at the DOS prompt.

What Do I Get? Interactive demo.

How Much? $49.95

How Do I Order? Velocity Development, P.O. Box 2749, San Francisco, CA 94126.

Velocity's stylized science-fiction sim *Spectre VR* seems like it's been around, in one incarnation or another, for some time. The latest, *Spectre VR*, is an interesting journey in a souped up, wireframe-type virtual world where killing robots and capturing flags are the order of the day. For a time, *Spectre* was the hottest game on Mac, and now it's finally available on PC.

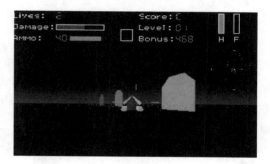

Spectre VR is set in "the cybernet," and puts you in control of a customizable attack vehicle known as (you guessed it) a "spectre." You can tailor the speed, shield configuration, and armaments of your vehicle to make it better suited to the type of game you're playing. For the single-player game, you simply zip around the cyberworld collecting flags and blasting 'bots, although more difficult robots and better weapons are automatically introduced as you progress through the levels. There are numerous hazards, such as acid, ice, and cybermud, to make things a little more tricky. Along the way, you can pick up anti-grav packs, enabling you to hover, and invulnerability shields, which deflect anything fired at the front of your spectre. All these elements vary for one-player games, meaning you can come back and play solo with some level of freshness.

However, the sparse graphics and lean sound make for limited appeal in solo play mode. The true strength of *Spectre VR* lies in its network and modem play capabilities, which allow you to play against numerous human opponents at the same time. Once jacked into the net, game play is so fast and furious that you'll forget about the wire-frame graphics and just work on staying alive. There are also play variants, such as soccer and tag games, to keep the challenges fresh. *Spectre VR* proves just how much network play options add to a game with only average graphics, and if you're wired in a net, this is one you'll definitely want to try.

Out of this World

Who's It From? Interplay/Delphine Software

Where Is It? X:\DOSDEMO\OOTW

How Do I Use It? Type AWDEMO at DOS prompt.

What Do I Get? Interactive DOS demo

How Much? Available on *Interplay's 10 Year Anthology,* with nine other games, for $59.99.

How Do I Order? Interplay Productions, 17922 Fitch Ave., Irvine, CA 92714. (800) INTERPLAY.

Out of this World is an older title, and I almost didn't include it for that reason. But then I took out my copy and dusted it off, discovering that it still holds up pretty well despite being eclipsed graphically by games like *Alone in the Dark* and *Flashback. Out of this World* was one of the first games to really use polygon rendering to make human figures move more fluidly, and as such it's a ground-breaking title. While most games were moving toward big, flashy graphics, *Out of this World* instead offered only 16 colors. It more than compensates for this by creating an effective illusion of interactive cinema, featuring smooth animation, lifelike human motion, and cinematic editing techniques to enhance the action sequences.

Since this is a puzzle-adventure-action game, the story isn't overly complex or, for that matter, logical. As a result of an experiment gone haywire, you have been zapped to an unknown world: it could be another planet, another dimension, or a futuristic landscape. In no time at all, you find yourself imprisoned, navigating a large maze, meeting people, and battling large centipedes, mountain lions, humanoids, and all manner of things out to get you. This may sound like traditional game fare, and, well, it is. But with its smooth-scrolling background, cinematic cuts, and landmark animation techniques, *Out of this World* becomes something more: a virtual movie, quite possibly the first of its kind.

Out of this World is currently available as part of *Interplay's Ten Year Anthology Classic Collection,* which also features *Wasteland, Dragon Wars, Star Trek: 25th Anniversary* (sans narration), *Castles, Lord of the Rings* (sans narration and cinematics), *The Bard's Tale, Tass Times, Battle Chess* (original version), and *Mindshadow* all on one CD-ROM for a reasonable price.

There's another reason to check out the original *Out of this World*: the sequel, *Out of this World 2*, is due out soon, and if the first title is any indicator of quality, we can expect some more solid gameplay.

Flashback

Who's It From? SSI/Delphine

Where Is It? X:\DOSDEMO\FBACK

How Do I Use It? Type FB at DOS prompt.

What Do I Get? Interactive demo of

commercial release.

How Much? $49.95

How Do I Order? SSI, 675 Almanor Ave., Ste. 201, Sunnyvale, CA 94086-2901. (800) 245-4525.

After scoring big with *Out of this World*, French developer Delphine pushed adventure gaming even further with *Flashback*. Never had a character in a game moved this smoothly. Standing, running, jumping, climbing, rolling, firing a gun: all are rendered in smooth, flowing sideview animation with occasional close-ups and cinematic cutscenes. Centered around a plot freely lifted from John Carpenter's *They Live*, *Flashback* concerns a pair of glasses created by your character, Conrad. These glasses, which allow the wearer to determine molecular densities, give Conrad a glimpse of something no one wants him to see: that certain important people are not actually humans, but merely aliens disguised as humans. It's not long before the aliens learn that Conrad knows their secret, so they wipe his memory and throw him in prison.

The game begins with Conrad escaping on a space-bike only to crash-land in the jungle. A message on a holocube directs him to New Washington, but first he must pick his way through a series of traps and pesky guards with only his agility and a pistol. A combination of arcade-type dexterity and problem-solving skills are necessary to get Conrad through all the various levels and places he has to go in order to regain his memory and undo the aliens' nefarious schemes.

While the jaw-dropping fluidity of movement is what makes *Flashback* instantly appealing, its fast pace and intelligent design help *keep* it appealing. More than just pretty pictures, *Flashback* is a clever, involving, action-packed game with just the right mixture of arcade play and adventure gaming. This is an interesting title, and it holds up well a year later. Joe Bob says check it out.

Xatax

Who's It From? Pixel Painters

Where Is It? X:\DOSHARE\XATAX

How Do I Use It? Type XATAX at DOS prompt.

What Do I Get? Episode 1.

What Am I Missing? Episodes 2 & 3.

How Much? $20.00

How Do I Order? Pixel Publishers, P.O. Box 2847, Marrifield, VA 22116. (703) 222-0568.

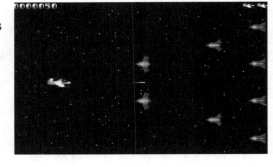

As you can see by their prominence in this chapter, scrolling space shooters are a popular game for shareware developers. Not all are created equal, but some are certainly more fun and worthwhile than others: *Raptor*, *Mutant Space Bats of Doom*, and *AstroFire* are good examples.

Xatax is another slick astro-shooter. Somewhat unique in the fact that it scrolls from right to left, it also features decent graphics and music, ground targets, and a wide variety of enemy ships. Control is familiar: arrow keys for movement, CTRL to fire, ALT to release a bomb. When some enemy ships explode, they release a wide variety of ship enhancements which you can pick up and use right away. These include powerups, rapid fire, missiles, extra lives, shields, "pods" (a drone ship that flies next to yours and fires when you do), and bombs.

I found myself getting nailed pretty frequently, which is a fair sign of replay-ability. If you like space arcade games, give it a whirl.

Kiloblaster

Who's It From? Epic MegaGames

Where Is It? X:\DOSHARE\KILO

How Do I Use It? Type KILO at DOS prompt.

What Do I Get? Volume 1: Death of a Starship, with 30 levels.

What Am I Missing? Volume 2: No Way Out and Volume 3: The Final Battle, featuring 30 levels each.

How Much? $30

How Do I Order? Epic MegaGames, 354 NE Greenwood Ave., Ste. 108, Bend, OR 97701-4631. (800) 972-7434.

Those nasty aliens are at it again. This time they're planning on conquering earth, and in order to keep you from interfering, they've sent your ship—the Starship Kiloprise—somewhere to the limits of outer space. With the ship broken down and most of the crew dead, you take a fighter jet and set out to warn your people of the coming invasion. This story is basically an excuse to line you up at the bottom of the screen and start shooting. Enemy ships attack you at increasing speeds in this straightforward arcade game, with some helpful power-ups and shields to be found along the way.

Jetpack

Who's It From? Software Creations

Where Is It? X:\DOSHARE\JET

How Do I Use It? Type JETPACK at DOS prompt.

What Do I Get? The first ten levels.

What Am I Missing? 90 more levels, save game feature, level editor.

How Much? $22

How Do I Order? Software Creations, 26 Harris St., Clinton, MA 61510. (508) 368-8654.

You're a daring young adventurer in search of gems, with only a jetpack and phase shifter to help you out! Like most side-view arcade games, *Jetpack* is a simple quest for more levels. Using the ALT key to thrust your jet pack and the CTRL key to fire your phase shifter, you traverse the many multi-tiered levels searching for

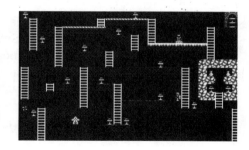

Jetpack Levels

Jetpack's level editor is a fav among gamers, who have created and uploaded countless levels throughout the years. We've included a few in X:\DOSHARE\JETPACK\LEVELS. They work with the registered version.

precious stones and fuel for your pack. Teleporters zap you to other places on the current level, and barriers can be moved by hitting the colored buttons or stepping on floor plates. Avoiding killer robots and other threats while you gather your riches and head for the exit to the next level is the point and challenge of *Jetpack*. Though no more or less challenging than many games of this type, *Jetpack* is quite noteworthy for the level editor that comes with the registered versions. *Jetpack* levels are a popular item on BBSs throughout the country, and a legion of loyal followers keep uploading more.

Invasion of the Mutant Space Bats of Doom

Who's It From? Pop Software

Where Is It? X:\DOSHARE\BATS

How Do I Use It? Type BATS at DOS prompt.

What Do I Get? 21 playable levels.

What Am I Missing? 64 levels.

How Much? $14

How Do I Order? Pop Software, P.O. Box 60995, Sunnyvale, CA 94088. (408) 450-3022. CIS: 71460,2432.

Along with *Raptor*, the other big scrolling space shooter of the year, *Invasion of the Mutant Space Bats of Doom* shows that a lot can still be learned from the old coin-op space games. While *Raptor* is undoubtably the better-looking game, *Bats* plays faster, costs less, and will run on most systems with ease.

In the tradition of *Galaxian*, *Bats* is a simple arcade-style space game where the better you do the harder it gets. Swarms of space bats of various sizes, colors, shapes, speeds, and strengths swoop toward you in weird, twisting patterns. When you clear the screen, you get still more bats, coming faster, and zigzagging in dizzying formations. You steer your simple ship in all four directions with the arrows keys, firing with the spacebar and dodging out of the way before a kamikaze bat takes you out. You get a free ship every time you reach the score shown in purple below your current score. There's even a two player mode!

Keep an eye on those bats as you're killing them. Many carry power crystals with them, and when you kill one of these bats, it releases its power crystals. Steer your ship over these crystals to get special powers depending on what color the crystal is.

Mutant Space Bat Color Key	
Green:	Makes your shots faster
Red:	Alternately makes your shot-spread wider or enables another gun
Blue:	Slows down enemies
White:	Turns all your enabled guns into MEGA guns
Purple:	Collect six and you get a free ship

The Lost Vikings

Who's It From? Interplay

Where Is It? X:\DOSDEMO\VIKINGS

How Do I Use It? Type VIKINGS at DOS prompt.

What Do I Get? Playable demo.

How Much? $15.95

How Do I Order? Interplay Productions, 17922 Fitch Ave., Irvine, CA 92714. (800) INTERPLAY.

The Lost Vikings, like the inestimable *Lemmings* before it, puts you in control of people with individual skills and *dares* you to make them work together to solve a level. Instead of controlling a truckload of impersonal little critters who have the annoying tendency to get squished and blown up, however, you're put in command of three obnoxious, loud- 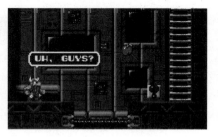 mouthed, nose-picking Vikings, who have been beamed aboard an alien intergalactic zoo. Are we having fun yet?

The interface is a weird cross between *Commander Keen* and the aforementioned *Lemmings*. You have total control over all three Vikings. Each one has his own unique ability, like jumping, blocking, or attacking, and the game can only be solved by using all three characters. If you need to get Erik the Swift to a high ledge, for example, he'll need to use Olaf the Stout to give him a boost. If you're stuck with one Viking, hit CTRL and see if the other two can offer some help.

It goes without saying that *The Lost Vikings* is a "cute" game. Each Viking is cartoonishly animated (try leaving them alone for a few minutes and see what they do), and when your Vikings die, they float off in a flaming boat to Valhalla. Oh, there are some nits to pick: if one of your Vikings dies, it's back to square one, even if the remaining Vikings make it to the level's exit, and there's no in-game save. Still, platform gamers will find much to amuse.

Ms. Chomp

Who's It From? Peter Siamidis

Where Is It? X:\WINGAMES\ MSCHOMP

How Do I Use It? Run MSCHOMP.EXE in Windows.

What Do I Get? The whole thing

How Much? Free

How Do I Order? Write with comments to gateway@cd.mcgill.ca.

This is just a bit of nostalgia, here primarily for historical purposes. Remember *Pac Man*? *Ms. Pac Man*? Well, this isn't it, but it's close enough to give you an idea of what all the fuss was about. I'm still not sure why *Pac Man* took off the way it did, but it did, and became one of the pivotal games in electronic entertainment.

The concept of *Ms. Chomp* is the same as in *Pac Man*: steer the little muncher around the mazes and gobble up all the dots. Power-ups are available for going after the ghosts and...well, you know the rest.

Watch Out Willi!

Who's It From? Chris Nokleberg

Where Is It? X:\WINGAMES\WILLI

How Do I Use It? Run WILLI.EXE in Windows.

What Do I Get? Eight worlds.

What Am I Missing? Five more worlds.

How Much? $10

How Do I Order? Chris Nokleberg, 4315 Norris Rd., Fremont, CA 94536.

The sound isn't so good, and for that matter neither are the graphics, but this little variation on the *Pac-Man* theme has some interesting puzzle solving elements that make it worth a look. Willi chews his way across various mazes, moving blocks in certain ways to get by while mowing as much grass as possible. Plus, there's an edit mode for creating your own puzzles! An amiable little bit of fluff.

Lode Runner: The Legend Returns

Who's It From? Sierra On-Line/Dynamix and Jeff Tunnel/Presage Software

Where Is It? X:\WINGAMES\LODERUN

How Do I Use It? Run LODERUNN.EXE in Windows.

What Do I Get? Interactive demo.

How Much? $49.95

How Do I Order? Sierra On-Line, P.O. Box 53250, Bellevue, WA 98015-3250. (800) 757-7707.

When it was first released, *Lode Runner* was more than just a game. It was an addiction. People simply couldn't get enough of what seemed mindless and repetitive to those who had never played before. A little man ran around a world, picking things up and making his way to the exit so he could get to the *next level*. What was so great about that?

You know, I have no answer to that question. I'm not quite sure why *Lode Runner* is so engrossing, and those who try to sit down for a brief game look up to find themselves still playing two hours later. It simply...*is*. You become the Lode

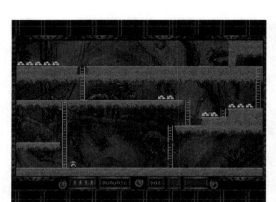

Runner, and you get so engrossed in the challenges that face him, that you simply *have* to see each level through to the end. And then the next level comes, and the next... It never ends. Jobs have been lost, marriages ruined, eyesight strained, all to steer a silly little man up ladders and across platforms to pick up stuff. Maybe it's the compulsion of solving what is in essence a puzzle of timing and movement. Maybe it's the fight for survival and victory. Maybe it's secret rays that the program emanates. Who's to know? Just be warned: *Lode Runner* is compulsively playable, and nearly impossible to tear yourself away from.

Having said all that about the original *Lode Runner*, it's time to let you know that *Lode Runner: The Legend Returns* is now available from Sierra On-Line for Windows. *LR: TLR* is a dangerous game. I was on deadline to finish this book, sat down to take a peek at the game, and lost three good hours of my work day. I looked up and the time was gone. This is just a mind-sucker of a game. The graphics are so sharp, the animations so smooth, the music and sound effects so good, and the levels so devilishly devised that once you begin, you can't stop.

In *LR: TLR*, you take control of Jake Peril, a little thief who races through a series of underground worlds to recapture the treasure of his people from the "evil empire." Each world is traversed by a series of single-screen levels made of ladders and platforms, and there are 15 levels in each world. Spread throughout each level are numerous types of treasure: what they are really doesn't matter, you just have to collect them all in order for the door to the next level to appear. Trying to keep Jake from succeeding are the Mad Monks: red-robed ghouls who chase him wherever he goes. If they catch him, they eat him. (*Gulp!*) Monks come in varying levels of intelligence and aggressiveness, and you can count on more difficult

---

New Levels!

For those who already have *Lode Runner: The Legend Returns*, we've included a selection of new levels designed by *LR* fans in X:\WINGAMES\LOADRUN\LEVELS. Just load them up and have a ball!

LODE RUNNER HINTS

- Goodies such as bombs, traps, and other stuff may be hidden beneath the turf. Blast away to see what you find.

- Blast several holes when monks are in hot pursuit. When—*if*—they get out of one, they'll fall in the next.

- You can't fire your blaster unless you have enough room. Make sure you stay at least one "Jake-length" away from wherever you're trying to shoot. The blaster does not work on the monks!

- Don't jump in a hole unless it's at least two—and preferably three—spaces wide. You won't be able to get out and you won't be able to shoot your blaster, so you'll be stuck.

and numerous monks to appear as you get further into the game.

Jake is armed with a little blaster that can temporarily blow holes in the turf. If a monk, or even Jake, falls into one of these holes, they usually can't get out again, and will be squished when the hole re-seals itself. There are other tools that Jake can find along the way, such as small delayed-action bombs that take out everything within their radius. Slime buckets can be used to slow monks down, mad monk snares will hang a monk upside down if he gets caught, jackhammers drill holes in surfaces the blaster can't penetrate, befuddlement gas makes the monks disoriented, the pickaxe can create cave-ins, and the darkness spotlight illuminates a small area around Jake when he's in the dark levels. There are also hideouts, where you can duck inside until a monk passes, and transports, which zap you to other areas of the level.

But there's more!!! Two players can play *Load Runner* together, either racing to see who gets the most gold first, or cooperating to defeat the monks. Plus, there's a full construction kit! You can build levels until you drop, putting as many monks, traps, goodies, treasure, or what-have-you wherever you want. There are so many good features in this package that I can't even list them all. There are numerous cheat options, slick animation scenes between worlds, the ability to jump instantly to any level, sharp MIDI music...everything about *Lode Runner: The Legend Returns* says "quality."

Space Pirates

Who's It From? American Laser Games

Where Is It? X:\ALG\SPDEMO

How Do I Use It? Type SPDEMO at DOS prompt.

What Do I Get? Interactive demo.

How Much? $59.95

How Do I Order? American Laser Games, 4801 Lincoln Rd. NE, Albuquerque, NM 87109. (505) 880-1718.

American Laser Games is undoubtably best-known for their laser-disk hit *Mad Dog McCree*: a popular arcade shooting game brought successfully to PC. Using live-action video, *Mad Dog* put you in the role of an old west gunslinger facing down the bad guys. Using the mouse to aim, you could shoot the other gunmen while trying to avoid innocent bystanders.

Well, ALG is bringing that same technology to bear with three new titles: *Mad Dog McCree II*, *Space Pirates*, and *Crime Patrol*. In *Space Pirates*, set in the year 3030, you play a Star Ranger commissioned by the Galactic Council to protect the galaxy from marauding privateers. These space-age pirates are constantly raiding ships and stealing cargo, wreaking havoc across the galaxy. The action begins with you on your way to a routine check of a new colony. Suddenly, you receive a desperate transmission from the captain of Colonial Star 1: his ship is under attack from the Black Dragon. Led by the notorious pirate Captain Talon, the Black Dragon has seized control of the powerful star splitter cannon. As the only Star Ranger in the area, you have to defeat Talon and his men and get the cannon back, or the entire galaxy will be in danger.

The mouse is used for all controls. To shoot your gun, just aim the crosshair at a target and click the mouse button. At the beginning of each game you have 10 phaser blasts, and can reload by clicking on the reload button in the lower-right corner of the screen. You can only shoot at two types of targets, pirates and innocent bystanders. If you hit the pirate before he gets you, the game continues. If you miss, or don't shoot fast enough, you lose a life. You also lose a life for shooting innocent bystanders. You only get three lives, so be careful out there!

Crime Patrol

Who's It From? American Laser Games

Where Is It? X:\ALG\CPDEMO

How Do I Use It? Type CPDEMO at DOS prompt.

What Do I Get? Interactive demo.

How Much? $59.95

How Do I Order? American Laser Games, 4801 Lincoln Rd. NE, Albuquerque, NM 87109, (505) 880-1718.

Like *Space Patrol, Crime Patrol* is a straight shooter using the mouse as a controller. Instead of assuming the role of a space ranger, however, you're part of various law enforcement teams, ridding the city of its criminals. In the full game, you start as a rookie cop, and progress to Undercover, SWAT, and ultimately, Delta Force. As with *Space Pirates*, the fight scenes become more  difficult as you advance to the higher levels, with more bad guys coming at increasingly faster rates, and more civilians in the way. Reflexes have to be quick, but your judgment has to be even quicker. Nail a civilian, lose a life.

World Circuit

Who's It From? MicroProse

Where Is It? X:\DOSDEMO\WC

How Do I Use It? Type DEMO at DOS prompt.

What Do I Get? Interactive demo.

How Much? $42.95

How Do I Order? MicroProse Entertainment Software, 180 Lakefront Dr., Hunt Valley, MD 21030-2245. (410) 771-1151.

Racing games are getting steadily more sophisticated, and MicroProse's *World Circuit* led the pack. It was the first truly sophisticated racing sim to take the same care and attention with modeling automobile dynamics that's normally taken with flight models. It also offered an impressive array of features, settings, and difficulty levels, allowing drivers to have complete control over their automobile and environment.

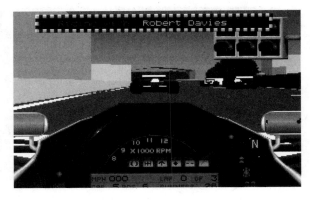

World Circuit tackles the high-speed Formula One racing cars, and does so not only with attractive graphics, but with a depth of play not seen previously, and only recently matched by *IndyCar Racing* from Papyrus. All manner of games are available: practice runs, quick-one shot races, non-championship racing events, and championship seasons. Complete control over the length of races, practices and qualifying runs, the level of difficulty and realism, the skill of opponents, and 16 different World Championship courses mean that you can jump right in and go at any time, or take a more studied and meticulous approach. Though there's only one car to drive, tires, gears, and wing settings can all be tweaked for better performance, sometimes making the crucial difference between winning and losing.

It's best to begin on Rookie mode, which has autobraking for turns, autoshifting, a "best-line" course to follow around the track, self-righting spins, and other training wheels. After practicing a bit to get the feel, you can start racing some of the pros (though their names aren't used here, since MicroProse couldn't get the rights) to see how you measure up. A full season involves qualifying rounds and practices to determine starting positions, and takes you through all the courses used in the World Championship races. It's a pretty tough campaign, but race fans won't want to miss the drama of qualifying, moving up the ranks, jockeying for position, and finishing out the entire season.

Visually, *World Circuit* may have been surpassed by *IndyCar Racing,* but its depth of play and auto modeling still hold up quite well. It'll also give you a taste for the forthcoming *World Circuit 2.*

SubWar 2050

Who's It From? MicroProse

Where Is It? X:\DOSDEMO\SUBWAR

How Do I Use It? Type DEMO at DOS prompt.

What Do I Get? Interactive demo.

How Much? $42.95 on floppy; $47.95 on CD-ROM.

How Do I Order? MicroProse Entertainment Software, 180 Lakefront Dr., Hunt Valley, MD 21030-2245. (410) 771-1151.

Aside from being the year of *Doom*-clones, 1994 was also the year of the submarine, with *SSN-21 Seawolf*, *Aces of the Deep*, and *Subwar 2050* all tackling different areas of underwater combat. *Subwar* postulates a future in which billion dollar subs are replaced by cheaper, faster craft more reminiscent of fighter jets than submarines. I originally labelled *Subwar* as "*Wing Commander* with bubbles," but it's become hugely popular, and is well thought-out and entertaining enough to warrant a look.

Based upon a futuristic scenario in which corporations looking for exploitable resources battle for control of the ocean floor, *Subwar 2050* casts you as a mercenary sub pilot. In the course of four campaigns, set in the North Atlantic, the Antarctic Ocean, the Sea of Japan, and the South China Sea, you are hired by various companies to protect their interests. This can involve anything from freeing trapped whales and escort missions, to destroying mining bases and intense close-in dogfights. Some missions have victory requirements that are merely puzzling without help. In "Save the Whales," for example, you have to destroy a "master control mine" to properly execute the mission. Without reading a hint file available on CompuServe, I never would have known this.

On the whole, however, *Subwar 2050* is an entertaining sim once you get the hang of it. Four different sub models are available throughout the course of the game, ranging from fighter subs to deep-sea and recon subs. Equipped with torpedoes, dumb-fire rockets, and decoys, your sub prowls the ocean floor, trying to remain undetected until it's close enough to unleash your weapons. With a "heads-up display" and front viewing window, the subs feel very much like fighter jets.

Using the "noise profile bar" to help ensure your sub is quiet enough, you travel close to the thermal level, slipping to the other side to hide from enemy sensors if the need arises. If you wind up with a torp on your tail, it's time to forget about stealth and start moving fast and turning tight to try to throw it off.

Featuring the standard MicroProse flight sim engine, a limited career mode, which allows you to rise through the ranks of combat; various theaters of combat; multiple views; and sharp polygon graphics, *Subwar 2050* is a refreshing change of pace from standard flight sims.

WARNING! This demo has no exit key! Once you're done, you'll have to reboot, so consider this before starting it!

Spear of Destiny CD-ROM

Who's It From? id Software and FormGen

Where Is It? X:\DOSDEMO\SPEAR

How Do I Use It? Type SOD at DOS prompt.

What Do I Get? Interactive demo,

featuring several playable levels.

How Much? N/A

How Do I Order? FormGen Corp.; 11 Holland Dr., Bolton, Ontario, Canada, (905) 857-0022.

If you're reading this book, it's a fair bet you probably don't need an introduction to *Wolfenstein 3D*. By now, you know that id's seminal first-person action game inevitably led to countless imitators, and, of course, to *Doom*. *Wolfenstein 3D* set the id pattern to follow: build a huge following with a hot shareware product, then release a retail product with the same

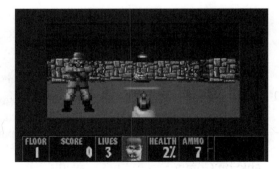

look, feel, and technologies, but also with all new levels and bad guys to attract the die-hard fan. That retail product was *Spear of Destiny*, and it just made a reappearance this summer on CD-ROM with two new mission disks filled with new levels.

Still controversial for its themes and violence, *Wolfenstein 3D/Spear of Destiny* casts you in the role of American soldier BJ Blazkowicz in the Second World War. You are given the unenviable task of penetrating deep into a Nazi castle to steal the "spear of destiny:" the spear used to pierce Christ's side while he was hung on the cross. Hitler believes the spear has supernatural powers, and the Allies want to demoralize him by taking it.

As you begin the game, you're given a hand gun and a clip, and must begin killing soldiers, collecting new ammo, getting your health back up after you're wounded, and finding the keys to get you to the next level. All of this prepares you for a final showdown brawl over the spear. You have a first-person window on this dark, moldering castle, so liberally adorned with Nazi symbols and pictures of Hitler that it was banned in Germany, where such symbols are illegal. Enemies charge at you right away, shouting curses in German and trying to kill you before you kill them. You blast away with whatever weapon is handy, spraying blood and body parts liberally across the stone corridors and rooms. There are secret passages to be found (look for old pools of blood or squished rats) and new and more dangerous Nazis to defeat.

After *Doom*, *SOD*'s once cutting-edge graphics look almost primitive and restrained by comparison, but there's no denying *SOD* still has plenty of gameplay value. With the two new sets of levels, *Return to Danger* and *Ultimate Challenge*, a level randomizer, and hint books, available both separately and in a "Super CD Pak," there are still plenty of enjoyable hours left in *SOD*.

Blackthorne

Who's It From? Interplay Productions/Blizzard

Where Is It? X:\DOSDEMO\ BTHORNE

How Do I Use It? Type BTHORNE at DOS prompt.

What Do I Get? Interactive demo with several levels.

How Much? N/A

How Do I Order? Interplay Productions, 17922 Fitch Ave., Irvine, CA 92714. (800) INTERPLAY.

Styled much like *Flashback*, Blizzard's *Blackthorne* provides terrific puzzle/action play with fluid motion and a healthy dose of blood to make things interesting. You assume the role of Kyle, the son of King Vlaros. The fantasy kingdom where the king rules is about to fall to the evil Sarlac, who is desperate to get his hands on the powerful Lightstone. Fearing what will happen if Sarlac can harness the power of the Lightstone, Vlaros sends Kyle to live among the humans, protecting the Lightstone and only returning when he is old enough to conquer Sarlac.

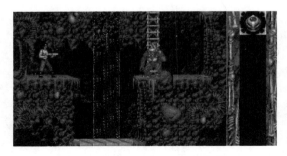

Does any of this matter in game-play? Not really, but it provides the action with some purpose and atmosphere as you blast the bad guys and figure out how to defeat each level. Kyle enters the dank caverns beneath Sarlac's keep with only a shotgun and quick reflexes. His hapless countrymen have been enslaved here, and many are dying or dead. Some mine, others are merely chained and beaten, and all (except for the skeletons) will be willing to help Kyle with each level as much as they can. Some will offer information, such as how to defeat the force fields or how things are often hidden behind waterfalls, while other actually provide "hover bombs" or healing potions. Kyle should talk to them all, and do his best to keep them out of the path of fire, since you don't want to kill them (at least not until you've found out whether they can be useful or not).

Control is slick and smooth, with right and left arrow keys controlling motion in either direction, the up arrow key used to climb up ledges and talk to prisoners, and the down arrow key used to climb down or crouch. While crouching, Kyle can perform a little tumble and come up ready to shoot: a good way to enter a

BLACKTHORNE KEYS

Certain functions change depending upon whether Kyle's gun is either sheathed or unsheathed. For example, he can't climb when the gun is unsheathed. Here's how the rest of the functions work:

Key	Weapon Sheathed	Weapon Unsheathed
S	Draws weapon	Sheaths weapon
Spacebar or F	Leap	Fire forward
D	Run	Fire backward
Q	Give up	Give up
E	Use object	Use object

blind area. If he's standing over an object, he can put it in inventory by crouching down. You can scroll through inventory functions with the PAGEUP/PAGE-DOWN keys.

Blackthorne is a worthy competitor to *Flashback*. Though the story is fairly standard role-playing fare, it works here to provide a good range of nasty monsters and a dread-filled atmosphere. As the levels grow increasingly larger and more complex, different sets of tasks must be performed to get through each, and solving tricky barriers keeps things challenging without interfering too much with the action (a fault that can be found in *Flashback* in certain places).

Rebel Assault

Who's it From? LucasArts Entertainment

Where is It? X:\DOSDEMO\REBEL

How Do I Use It? Type REBEL at the DOS prompt.

What Do I Get? Noninteractive demo.

How Much? $54.95

How Do I Order? LucasArts Games, P.O. Box 10307, San Rafael, CA 94912. (800) STAR WARS.

Imagine a game with all the best action sequences plucked from the *Star Wars* trilogy and you have *Rebel Assault* in a nutshell. In *Assault*, your character, "Rookie One," will fly a shuttle, an A-Wing, an X-Wing, a snow speeder, and will even need to blast Imperial troopers on foot in a captured Rebel base. Instead of the free, simulation-like movement of *X-*

Wing or *Tie Fighter*, *Assault* has you flying over tracks and movies played directly from the CD, and the result packs a visual punch that you won't find in the other *Star Wars* games. Divided into narrative "chapters," each involving arcade-like tasks and action sequences, *Assault* provides a more accessible game than its predecessors. It's clearly aimed at the entry-level gamer, and it has eschewed the fancy flight controls of the sims for a more arcade-like feel.

The quality of the video in the cut-scenes (there are a lot of them) has been reduced in order to play at full screen, but the result is a very decent frame rate and fast play even a single-speed CD-ROM drive. This is quite an achievement when you consider that the original orchestrated *Star Wars* music is simultaneously playing off the CD.

Be wary, however, as the control system leaves something to desired in earlier versions. If you wind up with v1.0 of *Assault*, you'll have to cope with spotty control and movement, and you'll need to re-calibrate the joystick after every one of the fifteen "chapters." Many of these problems, including sound-card support and numerous crashes, have been fixed in version 1.7

Rebel Assault does a better job of conveying the atmosphere of the *Star Wars* movies than any other LucasArts game.

Rebel Assault **Cheat**

To activate the *Rebel Assault* cheat mode, wait for the LucasArts logo to come up, then move the joystick up and press fire, move it down and press fire, left and press fire, and then right and press fire. You'll hear a voice say "LucasArts" if the mode enables.

You may then use numbers 1 through 9 to immediately jump to chapters 1 through 9, and letters A to F to go to chapters 10 to 15.

Hitting the plus (+) key in this mode will reset damage to zero.

TWO

CLASSICS, CARDS, PUZZLES, & SPORTS GAMES

What is a classic? That question raises heated debate in every area from books to music to movies. Some cite mass appeal, others simply longevity or even financial success. Many things are declared "instant classics," but the term is oxymoronic: to be a classic, something has to endure. It has to have staying power and almost has to take on a life of its own. It has to be discovered anew by each generation, who must recognize its value and hand it down to the next generation, and so on.

In the realm of games, classics are easy to define: they have endured for decades, often centuries, sometimes even millennia. Among classic games are such disparate titles as Senet, a spiritual game played by the ancient Egyptians as far back as 4000 B.C., and *Monopoly*, a game of money and real estate played throughout the world today. Each, oddly enough, says something about the values of the cultures that produced them: in Senet, you have to travel through the stages of death to reach the underworld, which is seen as a victory. In *Monopoly*, you have to drive the other players into bankruptcy, which is also seen as a victory. We do indeed live in interesting times.

For as long as civilization has existed, we have played. What did we play? "Race" games, such as pachesi and backgammon; wargames like chess and draughts (also known as checkers); games of position, such as Go (or Wei-Ch'i) and Nine-Men's Morris; and, of course, card games in so many varieties it takes one thousand-page books to list them all. Samurai took Go boards into battle and commenced play as soon as combat was over. Egyptians buried elaborate game boards with their pharaohs and painted tomb walls with numerous representations of nobles playing games. The earliest card games date to the Tang dynasty in China, around the seventh century. In African cultures, people dig Wari boards into the ground and play with small stones, as they have done for centuries.

These are all examples of "classics:" enduring games that people play and study and pass down. Whereas many of the games we've discussed so far will, in time, grow obsolete and be replaced by new and more elaborate variations, classic games maintain their integrity despite changing technology. By bringing classics like chess, backgammon, poker, and others to computers, we're continuing their traditions and adapting them for our own times. We are also adding substantially to their history, since computer games have made solitaire play possible in many classic games. The development of new and more complex artificial opponents is bringing chess, in particular, to a new level. Recently, Gary Kasparov lost the Intel Speed chess Grand Prix to the Pentium Genius2 computer—a sign that the artificial intelligence levels of chess computers are becoming tougher and tougher to crack.

So, in this chapter, you'll find some of the most popular games throughout history. Card games, in particular, feature prominently, but you'll also find board games, puzzles, trivia games, and casino-style games: enough to keep you busy for some time to come.

Canfield for Windows

Who's It From? Daniel Thomas

Where Is It? X:\WINGAMES\CANFIELD

How Do I Use It? Run CANFIELD in Windows.

What Do I Get? The entire game.

How Much? $17

How Do I Order? Daniel Thomas, 2301 North Huron Circle, Placentia, CA 92670. CIS: 72301,2174. Prodigy: CWRF01A.

Canfield is one of the most popular solitaire variants, and *Canfield for Windows* has become one of the most popular shareware titles of all time. Here's how it works:

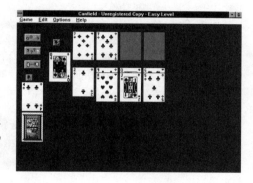

A pile of thirteen cards is turned face up to form the stock. The fourteenth card is dealt face up and placed in a top row to the right of the stock: this will be the first foundation. Four cards are dealt face up below the foundation row: these form your tableau. The rank of the remaining three foundations will be the same as the first foundation card, and you must build upon these foundations in the *same* suit, and in ascending order. You do this by building cards upon the tableau in descending ranks of alternating colors.

For example, you draw a three of spades as your first foundation card. The other foundation cards will be the remaining "threes" of the other suits, and you must build upwards on each suit: four of spades, five of spades, etc. You do this by building *descending alternating* suits (ten of clubs, nine of diamonds, eight of spades, seven of hearts, and so on) upon the tableau cards, moving the proper cards to the foundation as you're able. You deal three cards at a time into the talon (placing only the *top* card), or draw a card from the top of the stock. If you're able to place the top card of the three-card draw on the tableau, you can then try to place the next card, and so on.

Daniel Thomas's super *Canfield* program allows you to set levels for almost limitless cheating, so you can peek under cards to get just what you need. It also has a hint feature that points out good card placements, some small animations, undo buttons, and cartoon characters that pop in on your game now and then.

SOLITAIRE

Solitaire is, simply, any card game that can be played by one person. In terms of sheer number of variants, solitaire games outnumber all other kinds of card games. The goal is the same for each, though how one goes about it changes from game to game: get all the cards into a certain predetermined order, such as in suit sequence, alternating suit sequence, and so on.

Each game has certain elements in common. There is the *layout* of the cards as they are dealt on the table, which comprises the *tableau*, the *foundations*, and the *stock*. The tableau is simply the arrangement of the stacked cards in play, while the foundations are cards of a specific rank which must be built upon. The stock is a special pile of cards with various uses for various games, while the rest of the deck is simply called the *hand*. When a card is drawn from the pack and cannot immediately be put on either the tableau or the foundations, it is placed in a special pile known as the *talon*.

By drawing cards from the hand, you begin to build upon the face-up cards in the talon, looking to complete the foundations. For instance, your foundations may be all four aces, and you must build the suits consecutively among the tableau cards, moving them over to the foundations when able.

You didn't know solitaire was this complicated, did you?

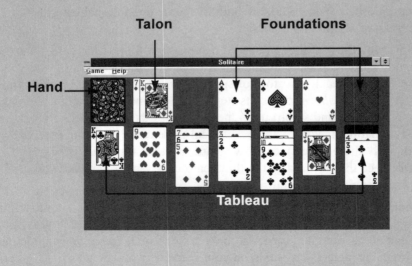

Talon   Foundations

Hand

Tableau

Spider Solitaire

Who's It From? John A. Junod

Where Is It? X:\WINGAMES\ WINSPIDR

How Do I Use It? Run WINSPIDR in Windows.

What Do I Get? The entire program.

How Much? $5

How Do I Order? John A. Junod, 3005C Greene Place, West Point, NY 10996.

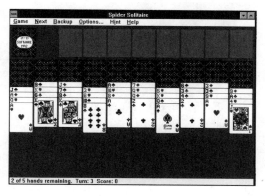

So you thought Canfield was tricky?

Spider, another solitaire variant, is played with two packs of fifty-two cards each. Ten cards are dealt face down in a row, and then three more rows are dealt face down on top of the first row. One card is dealt face down on the first four piles on the left (in Junod's enclosed *Spider Solitaire* game, these four are placed on alternating piles). A final row of cards is dealt face up on the piles, forming a tableau of 54 cards. There is no separate foundation, and all building is done right on the tableau.

Suits are built in decending order on the top card of any pile. For example: four of clubs, three of clubs, two of clubs, and so on. You begin building from the face-up cards in the tableau. When there are no possible moves left, you then deal *one* card to the top of each pile (ten cards altogether) and continue trying to build. The object is to assemble complete suits in sequences from ace to king. Once a suit is assembled, it can be removed from play. The game is only won if the entire pack is spent and two sets of four suits each are assembled.

Spider Solitaire is a smooth-working version of this classic game of patience. It doesn't have as many bells and whistles as *Canfield for Windows*—no animations or alternate deck designs—but it does offer several cheats (allowing for illegal card movements) and provides hints when you're stuck. Plus, Spider can be such a challenging solitaire game that it's refreshing to have a simple, "low-rent" (it only takes up about one-tenth of a meg) version for Windows.

Atlantic City Blackjack

Who's It From? Oleg Goldfayn

Where Is It? X:\WINGAMES\ BLACKJAC

How Do I Use It? Run BJ.EXE in Windows.

What Do I Get? The whole game.

How Much? $25

How Do I Order? Oleg Goldfayn, 2489 East Third St., Brooklyn, NY 11223. CIS: 71202,2013.

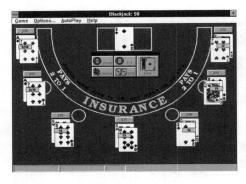

Atlantic City Blackjack ably combines the simplicity of blackjack with the excitement of casino betting. A Windows game, *ACB* is designed as a bird's-eye view of the traditional semi-circular casino blackjack table. There are places for seven players to sit, with a dealer at the center. Cards are dealt to each player in turn, and they may wager, hit, or stick. You control a player by clicking on the button at that player's spot, which places a bet. All the other players are played by the computer. There are options for displaying a running count of your cards and offering advice. A group of buttons allows control over all aspects of the game, including dealing, hitting, doubling, splitting, and standing.

A unique "autoplay" mode gives advanced players the option of viewing the "strategy tables" of the various players. You can check out each play-level, and practice against different styles of play. These tables are completely open for you to edit. Oleg is working on refining this feature even further.

A running total system would have been welcome in *ACB*, so that you could play as a single gambler with a set amount of money through a series of hands. Still, it's a fun and easy-to-use blackjack game for Windows.

BLACKJACK

Next to poker, blackjack (or twenty-one) is one of the most enduring gambling and card games. When it originally appeared two hundred years ago, it was played by both nobles and simple folk, and its simplicity and speed of play make it popular still. As a high-stakes gambling game, it is one of the most prominent found in modern casinos, where it is usually played at a semi-circular table and dealt from a "shoe" containing multiple packs of cards.

The players are dealt one card face down in rotation, followed by one card dealt face up in the same rotation. Each player must place an initial bet. Depending on protocol (such as whether or not there is a fixed or rotating dealer), players can bet first and then look at their card, or look at their card and then bet or fold. The dealer can then double the bets, the players redouble, and so on.

The object of each hand is to reach twenty-one or get closer to twenty-one than any of the other players without going over. All you have to do to win, however, is *beat the dealer*. There are no "ranks" as such in blackjack, and each card has only a numerical value. Face cards count as ten, while aces count as either one or eleven, depending upon the needs of the player. If players have twenty-one upon dealing (known as a *natural*), they are instantly paid out of the pot. If no one has a natural, players can request that additional cards be dealt into their hands to get closer to twenty-one. This is called *hitting*, and players hit until they are satisfied with their hands and decide to *stand*, or until they go *bust* (ie, over twenty-one). If you are dealt two cards of equal value, you can choose to *split* the hand, which means you can play each card as a separate hand with its own bet.

Some other tips are:

- If you have a count of fourteen or over, and the dealer has a face-up card lower than eight, it is a good idea to stand.

- Stick on fifteen or more.

Casino Twenty-One

Who's It From? Pyramid Software Development

Where is It? X:\WINGAMES\ CASINO

How Do I Use It? Run CASINO21.EXE

in Windows.

How Much? $19.95

How Do I Order? Pyramid Software Development, 2651 Sunset Blvd., #903, Rocklin, CA 95677-4242.

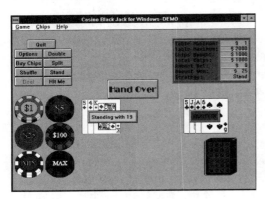

Pyramid's *Casino Twenty-One* is a good, full-featured shareware blackjack game with all the functions you could possibly want. You bet $1, $5, $25, $100, table minimum or table maximum by clicking on the chips on the left hand side of the screen. You deal, hit, split a hand, or stand by using the buttons just above the chips. An animated deck deals out cards to you and the dealer, and each hand ends by toting up the cards and announcing the winner. Chips can be bought in increments of $1000, and the computer tracks your wins, losses, bets, and remaining funds. There are settings for everything from table minimums and maximums to double-down betting. The game even offers you a cocktail!

Draw 5 Video Poker

Who's It From? AT-Ware

Where Is It? X:\WINGAMES\DRAW5

How Do I Use It? Run DRAW5 in Windows.

What Do I Get? The whole program.

How Much? $22.50

How Do I Order? AT-Ware, 720 Sunrise Ave., #28, Roseville, CA 95661-4815.

Draw 5 is an easy-to-use poker game working with "Jacks or better" rules (see "Poker" sidebar). To play, you just set the amount you wish to bet by clicking the proper icon, which raises or lowers the amount by ten dollars. You draw from an

POKER

Poker is the most popular card game in the world, bar none. Its many variants have emerged from smoky backrooms and saloons to become a socially acceptable pastime for millions of Americans. Though different players—and different countries—all have their own rules and variations, the basic premise of all poker games is the building of valuable "structures" of cards. Two or more of a kind, cards in sequence, and hands of matched suits are all poker structures with values in play.

In the most prominent versions of poker, five cards are dealt to each player, one at a time, in rotation. (Other versions may contain more or less cards, different value systems, or different procedures.) Players may decide which cards to build upon, and discard the rest. They are then dealt the same number of new cards as they discarded. Based on what they receive in this second deal, they may either have a viable hand, or they may fold. If the hand is good, or if they feel they can bluff the other players into folding, they can stay in the game without saying anything. They may raise the stakes by doubling their bets, forcing other players to either match that bet or raise it even further to stay in the game. If the hand is not good, or the player feels the pot is getting too rich, he or she can fold.

Here are some winning hands, ranked according to value (royal flush beats a straight flush, and so on):

- Royal Flush: An ace, king, queen, jack, and ten of the same suit.

- Straight Flush: Five sequential cards of the same suit.

- Four of a Kind: Four cards of the same rank.

- Full House: Three cards of one rank and two cards of another.

- Flush: Five cards of the same suit.

- Straight: Five sequential cards of different suits.

- Three of a Kind: Three cards of the same rank.

- Two Pair: Two cards of one rank and two cards of another.

- Jacks or better: Any single pair of jacks, queens, kings, or aces.
                     (House rules, used in *Video Poker for Windows*)

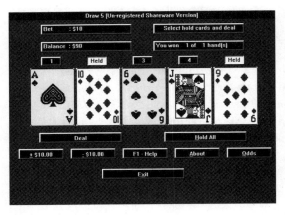

exhaustable supply of money ($100), so moderate your bets or risk going bust. (You *can* borrow money from the bank, however.) Deal a hand by clicking the Deal button, and then select which cards you want to hold by clicking on them. A small "Hold" designation will appear above each card, and you can then deal again to replace the discards. Following this second draw the program will evaluate your hand and tell you how much you've won or lost.

The controls are simple to use and the betting logical, but, like other shareware poker games, I never know what I'm losing to! Sorry, but if I lose on a pair of tens and a pair of twos, I'd like to know why. Other than that, *Draw 5* is a generally good poker program.

Windows Video Poker

Who's It From? Dean Zamzow

Where Is It? X:\WINGAMES\WINPOKER

How Do I Use It? Run WINPOKER in Windows.

What Do I Get? The entire program.

How Much? $15

How Do I Order? Dean Zamzow, 1171 Cordelia Ave., San Jose, CA 95129.

The look of this Windows poker game seems a bit cleaner and more attractive than *Draw 5*, but on the whole they're neck and neck for features. You choose a bet from 1-5, deal a new hand, click on the card you want to hold, and replace the discards by dealing again. As in *Draw 5*, I don't know what I'm losing *to*, however. It's like playing solitaire poker, and a bit disconcerting. I'm also not so sure about the betting system, which starts you at zero (talk about deficit gambling!) and goes in odd, non-monetary amounts. Still, it's attractively done and a good way to play a few hands when no one is around.

Battle Chess CD-ROM & Battle Chess 4000

Who's It From? Interplay	**What Do I Get?** Demos
Where Is It? X:\DOSDEMO\BC & X:\DOSDEMO\BC4000	**How Much?** BC CD-ROM: $79.95, BC 4000: $49.95
How Do I Use It? Type BC or BC4000 at the DOS prompt.	**How Do I Order?** Interplay Productions, 17922 Fitch Ave., Irvine, CA 92714. (800) INTERPLAY.

Interplay's first *Battle Chess* game was state-of-the-art when it was originally released, combining terrific animation with fun play. I remember delighting in the way the figures moved, especially the buxom Queen, who seemed to sashay across the board and gleefully melt opponents. At the time, we hadn't seen anything quite like that on computer, and it raised the computer graphics stakes to a new level. The anima-

Battle Chess CD-ROM

tions were so clever and so fluid that you forgot that the "combat" you were watching was essentially meaningless: it wasn't as if they were "fighting it out" to see who won the space. (The laws of chess had already determined that.) Still, it was heaps o' fun and certainly brought new life to an old classic.

Needless to say, Interplay stuck by their hit product, issuing new, even better versions, including the latest permutations, *Battle Chess CD-ROM* and *Battle Chess 4000*. The most recent *Battle Chess* features sharp high-res graphics and, on the CD-ROM version, a complete, narrated tutorial. Play can be configured for whatever difficulty level you like, and the AI seems to be pretty strong. *Battle Chess 4000*

CHESS

No board game has ever developed as strong a following or generated as much literature as chess. Though its origins are somewhat clouded by controversy, most believe it originated in India about 1500 years ago. The game of chess achieved its current form (and the pieces their current shape) sometime in the fifteenth century, when most of the rules we now know—such as the movement of the pieces, the *en passant* capture, castling, and so on—were generally accepted.

Make no mistake: chess is a wargame. The goal is to capture the opposing king. To do this, you use your pieces to invade enemy territory and manuever into a position of "checkmate," where the king cannot escape. It is played on a checkered board of eight squares by eight squares, their colors alternately white and black. The horizontal rows are called the rank, and the vertical the file. Players sit opposite each other, each controlling sixteen pieces, either white or black. They alternate moving according to the rules (see below), with white moving first.

Each player is given the same type and amount of pieces. In the following list, the name of the piece is followed by how many each player receives and how each may move and capture.

PIECE	NUMBER	MOVEMENT
Pawns	8	On its opening move, each pawn has the option of moving one or two spaces along the file. After the first move, a pawn may only move one space along the file. The only exception to this is when a pawn is performing a capture, in which case it can move one space on either *diagonal*. (A pawn can *only* capture on the diagonal.) If a pawn moves two spaces on an opening move, and if in moving only one space it will certainly be captured, that pawn is said to be captured *en passant*, or "in passing."

Rook	2	A rook may move any number of spaces along the rank and file.
Knight	2	A knight moves a combination of three spaces on either a rank or file, and then another space at a perpendicular angle to the first three space. This forms an "L" shape, and it may be made in any direction as long as the knight makes the *entire move* (ie: he cannot make just part of the move, such as three spaces down).
Bishop	2	The bishop can move along the *diagonal* in any direction, any number of spaces.
Queen	1	The queen can move any number of spaces in any direction, and is the single most powerful piece.
King	1	The king can only move *one* space in any direction, except when "castling." Castling can be performed once in any game, when both the rook and the king are in their initial position and there are *no* intervening pieces. A king can then move *two* spaces toward the rook performing the castle, followed by the rook assuming the space *passed over* by the king.

features silly futuristic figures and animations. The interesting thing about *BC 4000* is its use of "claymation"-style animation, which gives the pieces an added depth and a wholly unusual look. It is available in both VGA and SVGA graphic modes.

GNU Chess

Who's It From? Daryl K. Baker

Where Is It? X:\WINGAMES\CHESS

How Do I Use It? Run CHESS in Windows.

What Do I Get? The complete game.

How Much? Freeware

How Do I Order? Comments can be sent to dkb@mitre.org.

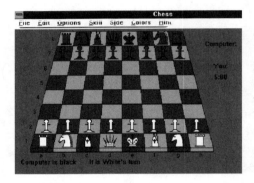

GNU Chess is a simple yet powerful and quite popular shareware game for Windows. For such a small program, there are options galore, from changing the color of board and pieces, to movement clocks, time limit settings, side switching, takebacks, *en passant* captures, and hints. There is a board setup command, which allows you to set up a game any way you choose: an important tool for those studying classic strategies and past games. The artificial opponent seems pretty darn good, and to see just how it works, you can display search statistics and watch as it goes through all the possible moves. It can also be set for different levels, and you can even designate the "search depth." This means that you can set the exact number of stored moves the AI can run through before it picks one. The more it searches, the longer it takes and the more likely it is for the AI to come up with a good move. *GNU Chess* is an altogether solid little piece of work, and while it won't win any awards for beautiful graphics, it has depth where it counts. There are also numerous text files with lines of code, and the code appears completely editable, which means you can hack it if you like. As far as I can tell, it's freeware, so have at it.

IGO

Who's it From? David Fotland and Roger White

Where is It? X:\DOSHARE\IGO

How Do I Use It? Type IGO at the DOS prompt.

What Do I Get? Tutorial with 9 X 9

beginner game board.

How Much? Free

How Do I Order? More advanced programs can be ordered from Ishi Press International, 76 Bonaventura Dr., San Jose, CA 95130. (408) 944-9900.

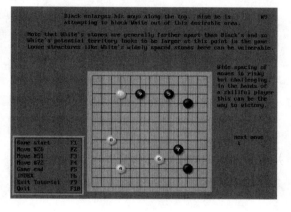

One writer has aptly described Go as the equivalent of five simultaneous games of chess—one at each of the four corners and one in the middle—with the added complexity of each game affecting the other. I could go on at some considerable length on how to play Go, since I have only given the most basic introduction to this complex and challenging game (see sidebar). Since space is limited, however, I'll refer you to *IGO*.

Roger White, of the American Go Association, introduced me to this terrific, beautifully designed little introduction to Go as I was working on this book. It was created to teach people new to Go all the concepts and fundamental elements of the game through an illustrated tutorial, working from the simplest rules up to slightly more complex strategies, and a walk-through of a sample game. A scaled-down 9 X 9 game board with a complete (albeit easy-to-beat) artificial opponent allows the user to play through small games and get the feel for Go. The graphics are terrific, and as an introduction to Go it can't be beat.

When players have a thorough understanding of the game, they can move on to Fotland's major program: *The Many Faces of Go,* which features the best AI routines, a complete board to play on, and more. For more information on Go, contact the American Go Association at P.O. Box 397, Old Chelsea Station, New York, NY 10113.

GO

I have recently become utterly fascinated with the ancient and complex Asian game of Go, as it is known to the Japanese (or Wei-ch'i, as the Chinese call it). The earliest references to it date as far back as 625 B.C. in China, but it is quite probably older than that. Go eventually made its way to Japan, where it was passionately embraced in court circles. It was soon played by samurai and commoner alike, and state institutions devoted to its study and teaching sprouted up throughout Asia. Professional Go masters still make a substantial living, and are ranked according to their skill. Today, many Asian newspapers carry Go columns, much like American papers carry chess or bridge columns, and the game is slowly penetrating the west. Go clubs can be found in surprising numbers throughout America, and the American Chess Master Edward Lasker has predicted that it will eventually supplant chess as the leading intellectual game of the West.

Go is a game of territorial capture involving black and white discoidal pieces, traditionally known as *stones*. These stones are placed on a square board of 19 by 19 lines, forming 361 intersections. Players alternate placing stones on the intersections of the lines—*not* on the spaces—with black moving first. Nine of these intersections are marked with circles, and these are used for "handicapping" purposes, in which weaker players are given a certain number of starting stones to give them an advantage. Any stone or group of adjoining stones that is *completely* surrounded by an opponent's pieces, so that there are *no free* adjoining intersections, is said to be dead, and is removed from the board. The object of the game is to mark off territory with an impregnable "wall" of stones, so that you control the vacant points of the board in such a way that they cannot be occupied by the enemy. The player controlling the most *open* territory at the end of the game wins.

For example, in the illustrations at the right (from IGO), the white stone is surrounded on three sides by black. It retains one "liberty," which is marked by the letter C. If black places a stone on this liberty, then white is said to be "dead" and is removed from play.

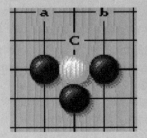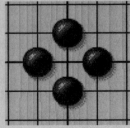

TurboGo

Who's It From? Arnoud van der Loeff

Where Is It? X:\DOSHARE\ TURBOGO

How Do I Use It? Type GO at the DOS prompt.

What Do I Get? The whole shebang.

How Much? Free (public domain).

How Do I Order? Write with comments and suggestions to Arnoud van der Loeff, Wilhelminastraat 159-3, 1054 WD Amsterdam, The Netherlands.

Arnoud van der Loeff's superb public domain program, *TurboGo*, is a powerful program for beginning players. *TurboGo* has a wealth of options, such as alternate board sizes (for practice games and novices) and move take-backs. The AI seems pretty strong, though I'm sure a Go Master would surely find the problems with it. Still, for those just getting into Go, this is a good introduction to some of the basic concepts and strategies. Play with it for awhile and see what you think, then go out (no pun intended), get a nice Go set, and hunt down some good introductory books to get you started.

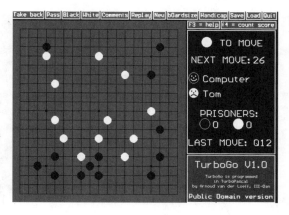

Backgammon

Who's It From? George Sutty, Graphics Software Labs

Where Is It? X:\WINGAMES\BG

How Do I Use It? Run BG.EXE in Windows.

What Do I Get? The whole game.

How Much? $15

How Do I Order? George Sutty, 79006 Moonmist Circle, Huntington Beach, CA 92647.

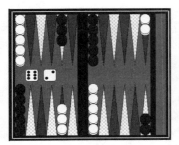

George Sutty's *Backgammon* is a good, basic example of a workable backgammon game for computer, with a series of simple mouse clicks to roll the dice, move pieces, and pass play onto the opponent. There is a "suggest move" function as well as the ability to score numerous games against the computer and set the difficulty level. Simple but effective.

BACKGAMMON

Backgammon is another ancient board game, believed by many to have preceded chess. It is played on a rectangular board marked with twenty-four triangles (or *points*) of alternating colors. The spine, or *bar*, of the board separates the two halves of the board. Each player starts the game with fifteen checkers of opposite colors, a pair of dice, and a dicing cup. At the beginning of the game, the checkers are placed as shown in the figure above. The object of the game is for players to move all of their checkers to their "home board" (the side the player is sitting on), and then off the board.

Movement is based upon dice rolls, with each die constituting separate moves. For example, a roll of two and six would mean one checker moves two spaces, and one six, or one checker two spaces, and that same checker another six. Movement must be made onto open points and must be made in the proper direction: clockwise for black, counterclockwise for white. The goal is to be the first to get all your pieces off the board and into the pocket to the left. If a single piece is on a point, an opponent may capture that piece and put in on the bar. To escape, the player must roll a valid number that would place the piece on a point.

Double Match

Who's It From? Dan Puraty

Where Is It? X:\WINGAMES\ DBLMATCH

How Do I Use It? Run in DBLMATCH Windows.

What Do I Get? The whole program.

How Much? $12.00

How Do I Order? Dan Puraty, 3536 Kent Rd., Stow, OH 44224-4602. CIS Program Number 1029. CIS: 71563,1245.

Like *Concentration*, *Double Match* presents a board covered with squares, beneath which are pairs of pictures. By uncovering the pictures and matching the pairs, the squares are removed from the board to reveal a phrase. The first player who correctly guesses the phrase is the winner. Each player continues to uncover squares until a wrong match is guessed, and each correct match adds to the total points for that player. There are 27 matched pictures in all, as well as one "wild card" square, which matches any other picture chosen and reveals its pair as well. Each new game fills the playing board with random picture icons and score values. The phrase hidden behind the playing board starts with a value of $10,000, and is diminished with each correct match.

You can play up to four other players, or computer opponents, in *Double Match*. Be warned, however, that the computer opponents are as moronic as they come. I never saw one get more than a single match or two, and *never* had one solve a phrase. So, play with a friend, and don't forget to turn the sound off—it will drive you batty.

Jpuzzle

Who's It From? Sofia Systems

Where Is It? X:\WINGAMES\JPUZZLE

How Do I Use It? Run JPUZZLE in Windows.

What Do I Get? A basic working version with several features blocked out.

What Am I Missing? A wider selection of piece-numbers, future enhancements and bug fixes, and additional puzzles. For an extra $5 with registration, you can get a personalized puzzle of any photo.

How Much? $16 ($21 for one personalized puzzle, each additional personalized puzzle add $15)

How Do I Order? Sofia Systems, P.O. Box 360188, Milpitas, CA 95036. (408) 942-5401.

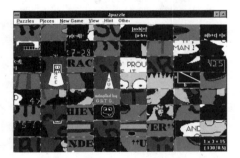

Computer jigsaw puzzles? Why not?

Sofia Systems' *Jpuzzle* is a Windows puzzle game that loads any .BMP file, scrambles it into anywhere from four to four hundred pieces, and challenges you to put it back together. There are two different modes for moving pieces in *Jpuzzle*: "jigsaw" and "sliding." In "jigsaw," you click on two pieces to exchange their positions, while "sliding" puzzles are trickier, featuring one empty position into which you can "slide" adjacent pieces. Sliders can be devilishly difficult, because you can't just "swap" pieces, you have to move them around the puzzle board to get them into position.

Jpuzzle provides hints and allows puzzles to be saved for completion later. It also keeps track of how many moves you make and how much time has elapsed. By selecting the "Picture" option in the View menu, you can peek at what the finished puzzle is supposed to look like. You can also stretch or shrink the picture by selecting "Size to Window." There are three bitmaps included, and you can import any bitmap into *Jpuzzle* and "puzzle-ize" it. I've even thrown in a couple myself: bitmaps of Buddha and Abraham Lincoln. Nothing quite like jigsaw puzzles that don't take up any table space!

Mah Jongg for Windows

Who's It From? Ron Balewski

Where Is It? X:\WINGAMES\MJ4WIN

How Do I Use It? Run MJWIN in Windows.

What Do I Get? The game with numerous tile sets.

What Am I Missing? More tile sets.

How Much? $20

How Do I Order? Ron Balewski, 412 E. Ridge St., Nanticoke, PA 18634-2915.

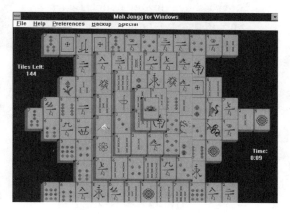

Ron Balewski's *Mah Jongg for Windows* is a beautiful and elegant version of yet another ancient game, this one predating Confucius. The game consists of a variety of tiles (see sidebar) laid out in a formation called a *Dragon*. The position of the tiles in a dragon is completely random, making each unique. Some are more difficult than others to play, and some are even impossible. The tiles are placed in stacks ranging in height from one tile at the edge to five tiles at the center.

The object of Mah Jongg is to remove all of the tiles in matching pairs. However, only tiles which are "free" can be removed. A free tile has nothing on top of it and it can slide out to the left or right (*not* to the top or bottom). If tiles on both sides are stacked to the same height the tile is not free to be removed. The only exception is with the Seasons and the Flowers, which cannot be matched identically. So any flower can match with any other flower, and any season can match with any other season.

To remove a pair of free tiles, first select one by clicking on it, then select its mate by clicking on it. If they match, they will be removed from play. A counter in the upper left hand corner tells you how many tiles are remaining in the dragon, and a clock counting down on the right keeps track of how long you're taking to solve the current dragon.

MAH JONGG

Here are some of the tips provided by Ron Balewski for helping solve a dragon:

- Concentrate on removing the four tiles which are blocking the most moves—the topmost tile, the single tile on the left, and the two tiles on the right.

- Look for quadruples. If all four of a given tile are free, remove them all immediately. This will get them out of the way and won't cause problems later.

- Keep an eye out for doubles (two tiles free) of tiles with only two left. These should also be removed immediately.

- Before removing two tiles of four remaining, be sure that you will leave no trapped tiles.

- Always check for triples. If you've found a pair with four remaining, see if any more are free. Then, take the two which will free up the most tiles.

There are 42 different tiles used in mah jongg in the following groups:

27 Suit tiles (nine tiles in each of three suits):
—The Suit Of Dots
—The Suit Of Bamboo
—The Suit Of Crak, or Characters

3 Dragons

4 Winds—North, East, South, and West

4 Seasons—Spring, Summer, Autumn, and Winter

4 Flowers—Orchid, Plum, Mum, and Bamboo

Spin 'n' Win

Who's It From? Dan Puraty

Where Is It? X:\WINGAMES\ SPINWIN

How Do I Use It? Run SNW.EXE in Windows.

How Much? $10.00

How Do I Order? Dan Puraty, 3536 Kent Rd., Stow, OH 44224-4602. CIS Program Number 1144. CIS: 71563,1245.

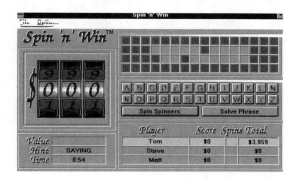

While Dan Puraty's *Double Match* was a version of *Concentration*, *Spin 'n' Win* is an amiable variant on *Wheel of Fortune*. In *Spin 'n' Win*, one to three players take turns spinning a numbered wheel and guessing letters to solve a phrase. At the beginning of each new game, the computer picks a random phrase, displaying it as letter blanks and offering simple "person, place, saying, or thing" clues.

Each player has the chance to spin the wheel or solve the phrase. If they spin the wheel, they can guess a letter, and if that letter is in the word, they get the amount they spun. If not, play passes to the next player. The current player continues to spin until the first wrong letter guess, then game control is passed to the next player. Scoring and play works based upon the spinner values as follows:

- $50 or less   Player wins a free spin for later use.
- $950 or more   Player loses turn, no score is made.
- $450 to $550   Player can pick a vowel, but no score is made.
- triple digits (111, etc)   Player goes broke.

Voodoo Doll for Windows

Who's It From? Diversions Software

Where Is It? X:\WINGAMES\ VOODOO

How Do I Use It? Run VOODOO.EXE in Windows.

What Do I Get? The whole thing.

What Am I Missing? If you register it, he promises not use his voodoo doll on you.

How Much? $5 (Cheap!)

How Do I Order? Ian Firth, Diversions Software, 966 Kramer Court, Aurora, CO 80010. CIS: 76450,3711.

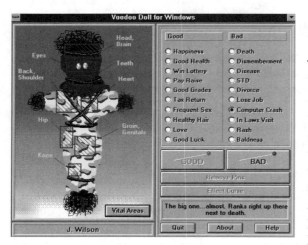

When I first heard about this, I thought it was so strange that I just *had* to find it and include it. Ian Firth's bizarre little program is *exactly* what it says it is: a voodoo doll for Windows. No bells, whistles or games. Upon starting it up, you are presented with a representation of a voodoo doll, with certain anatomical features highlighted. After entering the name of the person you wish to voodoo-ize, you can either work good voodoo (love, money, sex, health) or bad voodoo (broken health, financial ruin, veneral diseases, etc). Click on the "work voodoo" button and the screen does a little shimmy. Your spell is cast.

If you have any positive results with this, let me know! I have some publishers I'd like to try it on.

Brainteaser

Who's It From? Alan F. Shikoh, MD

Where Is It? X:\WINGAMES\BTEASER

How Do I Use It? Run BT.EXE in Windows.

What Do I Get? The whole program.

How Much? $5

How Do I Order? Alan F. Shikoh, MD, 1421 Briarcliff Ave., Charlottesville, VA 22903. (804) 979-0378.

Ever been to a rural restaurant and played one of those jumping peg games built from a slab of wood? You know the things: jump peg A over peg B to remove peg B from the board, until all but one are left. They leave 'em at your table so you don't notice how long it's taking to get your food.

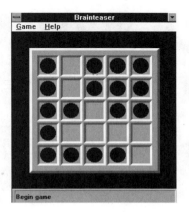

Well, Dr. Shikoh's *Brainteaser* works on much the same notion. There is one free space on a grid of 5 X 5, with the other spaces occupied by blue dots. You just click on one blue dot and drag it over another—horizontally, vertically, or diagonally—to remove it from the board. I'd offer some tips, but there really aren't any! Just start jumpin'!

Amnesia

Who's It From? Oscar Daudt Neto

Where Is It? X:\WINGAMES\AMNESIA

How Do I Use It? Run AMNESIA.EXE in Windows.

What Do I Get? The basic game.

What Am I Missing? Different board sizes and other options.

How Much? $25.00

How Do I Order? Oscar Daudt Neto, Rua Sebastiao Lacerda, 30/905-1, 22.240 Rio de Janeiro, Brazil.

Another variant of *Concentration*, this one has less of a game show feel and is more of a straight matching game. Here, you match pairs of flags on a grid. There's an elaborate scoring system, bonus time allowances, as well as numerous

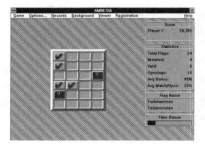

configuration options. The clock is always running so you can see just how fast you clear the board. With the registered version, you can select from different board sizes or two person play. There's even an online guide to the identities of all the flags.

EmPipe

Who's It From? Yutaka Emnu

Where Is It? X:\WINGAMES\EMPIPE

How Do I Use It? Run EMPIPE.EXE in Windows.

What Do I Get? The complete game.

What Am I Missing? Registration disables the nagging messages.

How Much? $10

How Do I Order? Yutaka Emnu 920-1, Hijaski-Hinatsuk, Tsukuba, Ibaraki, 305 Japan. CIS Product Number 612.

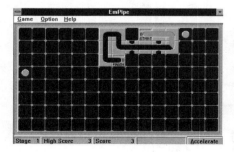

In *EmPipe*, you build a small pipeline to channel the flow of water through a grid. Each game starts with a beginning and ending point placed on a grid. By using differently shaped pipes—elbows, angles, straights—you create a meandering path from the point labelled "start" to the point labelled "end." At some point, water begins to start flowing, and as you progress through various levels, it begins flowing both sooner and faster. You have to build your pipeline before the water overtakes it, or you lose.

One trick is that not all pipes are available at once: you have to lay whatever pipe is offered in the turn, and if it's not one you want, you have to just lay it and change it later in order to go on. To make things more complex, the different configurations get trickier as you proceed, forcing you to build your pipeline through various numbered waypoints before winding up at the ending position. Plus, more and more "walls" start to show up, and you have to route your pipes around them. As the pace and complexity increases, this turns into quite a challenging little game. Well worth a look.

Crime Trivia

Who's It From? Dan Linton and Jason Blochowink

Where Is It? X:\DOSHARE\CRIME

How Do I Use It? Type CRIME.

What Do I Get? Basic game with 30 questions.

What Am I Missing? Classic Edition: 300 questions for $11.95, Deluxe Edition: 500 questions for $16.95, Gold Edition: 1000 questions for $21.95.

How Do I Order? Software Creations, 26 Harris St., Clinton, MA 01510. (508) 368-8654.

Which bank robber kept a white rabbit, often going out of her way to obtain lettuce for her pet?

Who was the presidential assassin who lived under the alias "O.H. Lee" prior to his crime?

Who was the prosecutor of the Manson family for the Tate-LaBianca murders?

These are just a few of the questions in this small sample of *Crime Trivia*, which features questions on everything from gangsters to assassins to mass murderers and serial killers. Being a true-crime buff, I found this program to be a lot of fun, though some of the questions go beyond the obscure to

become downright arcane. (How many questions can you ask about Leon Czolgosz, the man who assassinated President McKinley?) Only a scattering of questions are included here, but many, many, more (from 300 to 1,000) are to be found in the different versions of the game. Like many shareware trivia games, *Crime Trivia* was built using the Trivia Shell, which can turn a series of questions into a scoring trivia game.

How much sick knowledge is rattling around in your head? Check out *Crime Trivia* and find out.

Answers: Bonnie Parker, Lee Harvey Oswald, and Vincent Bugliosi.

Dominate

Who's It From? Shadoware

Where Is It? X:\WINGAMES\DOMINATE

How Do I Use It? Run DOMINATE in Windows.

What Do I Get? A working version of the game.

What Am I Missing? The ability to edit your own board.

How Much? $15

How Do I Order? Shadoware, P.O. Box 0155, New Port Richey, FL 34656-0155.

The battle for control of a playing board is central to numerous games, and indeed is the essence of most strategy gaming. From chess to Go, two players alternate moving, each in an attempt to outmaneuver the other. *Dominate* is from a strategy subgenre that boils play down to its simplest level, where pure move and countermove decide the victor. Each player controls a certain color piece, either green or red. Two of each piece start the game on opposite sides of the board, and the goal is to completely dominate the board by occupying the most squares before you run out of moves.

The rules are simple: each time you move one of your pieces to an adjoining square, that piece duplicates. In other words, the starting piece stays where it is and a new piece takes over the next square. You're allowed to move two spaces away, but when you do this *the pieces don't duplicate*. To add a combative twist, any piece that moves into a space adjoining any number of opposing pieces, converts the opposing pieces to its own color. For example, if red moves into a space next to three of your greens, those three greens become red, increasing the enemy's numbers and decreasing yours. There are numerous board configurations, with different walls and varying numbers of starting pieces. With registration, you can even edit your own board!

Hexxagon

Who's It From? Argo/Software Creations

Where Is It? X:\DOSHARE\ HEXXAGON

How Do I Use It? Type HEXX at the DOS prompt.

What Do I Get? The whole game.

How Much? $22

How Do I Order? Software Creations, 26 Harris St., Clinton, MA 01510. (508) 368-8654.

Hexxagon is a DOS game much like *Dominate*. (Which came first I'm not really sure.) It's based around hexagonal rather than square pieces and features a honeycomb-like grid to play on. The graphics have a more three-dimensional feel than those in *Dominate*, and on the whole the animations seem better, but there don't seem to be as many options for play.

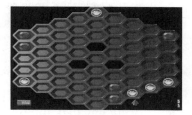

Pentominos

Who's It From? Stephen Balogh

Where Is It? X:\WINGAMES\PENT

How Do I Use It? Run PENT in Windows.

What Do I Get? The whole game.

How Much? $15 Australian

How Do I Order? Stephen Balogh, P.O. Box 414, Caulfield East, Melbourne, Australia 3145.

This is a very tricky puzzle game involving geometric pieces placed on a grid. Using a mouse, you select differently-shaped pieces from the bar along the top. The selected piece will "stick" to your mouse, and by clicking the right button you can rotate the piece in any direction. All the pieces along the bar fit together in the box at

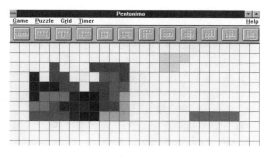

the center of the grid. Can you make them fit? It ain't nearly as easy as it looks.

Pinball Fantasies

Who's It From? 21st Century Entertainment

Where Is It? X:\DOSDEMO\PINBALL

How Do I Use It? Type PINBALL at the DOS prompt.

What Do I Get? Interactive demo.

How Much? $29.95

How Do I Order? 21st Century Entertainment, P.O. Box 415, Webster, NY 14580. (716) 872-1200.

Of all the pinball games to hit the market, 21st Century's *Pinball Fantasies* is undoubtably the best. It does a marvelous job of capturing the feel, speed, color, and sounds of a true pinball game. The CD-ROM version comes with eight different pinball tables, more digitized sounds, some really sharp music, and a complete multimedia history of pinball!

The version included here has one playable table: "Playland." Though it only has a 10-minute play limit, that should be more than enough to give you a feel for how fast and colorful this game really is. You can play as many balls as you like for the ten minute limit, but the game *will* kick out after ten minutes. To play, use the Down arrow to pull the plunger and release it to send the ball onto the board. The left and right hand Shift, CTRL, or ALT keys control the left and right flippers, and the Spacebar actually gives the machine a "nudge."

BreakThru

Who's It From? Spectrum-HoloByte

Where Is It? X:\WINGAMES\ BRKTHRU

How Do I Use It? Run BTDEMO.EXE in Windows

What Do I Get? Interactive demo

How Much? $29.95

How Do I Order? Spectrum HoloByte, 2490 Mariner Square Loop, Alameda, CA 94501. (800) 695-GAME.

Though *Tetris* inventor Alexey Pajitnov's name and grinning face are featured prominently on the box of this title from Spectrum-HoloByte, the game is in fact not designed by Pajitnov, but is the first in a line of titles inspired by his hugely successful puzzle games. *BreakThru* is an interesting twist on the *Tetris* theme. Rather than positioning falling blocks into the play area, the screen begins filled with blocks, and you have to

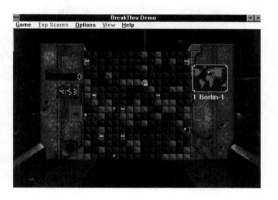

remove them all to win. The difficulty lies in the fact that there are four colors of blocks, and each can only be removed when it is adjacent to blocks of the same color. The blocks drop as you remove their supports, and the wall gets lower and lower. It may be easy at first, but it gets steadily harder as you try to clear off the entire screen. Plus, as you go on, there are obstacles to make things even more difficult. It's a game perfectly suited for the Windows environment, where it's easy to while away some time between applications with a little game of *BreakThru*. If *Tetris* hooked you as it did so many people, you'll want to check out *BreakThru*.

Hangem

Who's It From? Eric Jarrett

Where Is It? X:\WINGAMES\HANGEM

How Do I Use It? Run HANGEM in Windows.

What Do I Get? A working game.

What Am I Missing? The ability to alter the dictionary.

How Much? $7.50

How Do I Order? Eric Jarrett, P.O. Box 34749, Richmond, VA 23234.

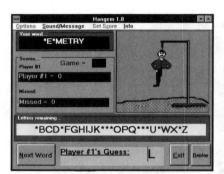

There are a lot of hangman-type games floating around out there, and many of them are surprisingly boring. Some don't even bother to draw a figure. Well, thanks to Eric Jarrett, we at least have a doodle-like picture to hang. *Hangem* is simple to use: just type in the letter you want to guess. If it's right, you're one letter closer to getting the word, if not, you swing. Registration gets you a version that allows you to edit the dictionary.

Bago

Who's It From? H.G. Wrekshun

Where Is It? X:\WINGAMES\BAGO

How Do I Use It? Run BAGO in Windows.

What Do I Get? The complete game.

How Much? Free

Once again, you never know when the smallest things will hook you. *Bago* looked like a simple enough diversion for a few minutes, but I soon found myself returning to it when I needed a break, and if you like word games, you will too. This is, quite obviously, *Boggle* for computer, but it's simple and flexible enough to make it work. You start each game with a "tray" filled with lettered blocks, and you have to use connecting letters to form words. The letters can connect horizontally, vertically, or diagonally, up or down, but must connect and must form a word four or more letters long. The computer plays along, its words hidden from view until the end, when it totes up the score. *Bago* isn't fancy, but like most word games, it doesn't have to be fancy to work.

Bandit

Who's it From? Wicked Witch Software

Where is It? X:\WINGAMES\BANDIT

How Do I Use It? Run BANDIT.EXE in Windows.

What Do I Get? A video slot machine.

How Much? Free.

How Do I Order? Send comments to Wicked Witch Software Company, P.O. Box 3452, Reno, NV 89505.

I see them in Atlantic City whenever I go to the casinos: row upon row of people—mostly elderly— feeding nickels, quarters and silver dollars into machines one after another. They plug their money in, pull the handle, and wait for the magic to happen. Three in a row means a hatful of money, but more often they come up lemons.

Same goes for our little one-armed *Bandit*. Hit the Play button and the wheels spin. Maybe they come up all cherries now and again, but not for me. Probably the simplest computer game ever made: one command is all you need.

Hey, why not? Bill Gates sits around playing *Minefield* in his off-hours, and *Bandit* could hardly be any sillier than that.

Cipher for Windows

Who's It From? Nels Anderson

Where Is It? X:\WINGAMES\CIFERWN

How Do I Use It? Run CIPHERWN.EXE in Windows.

What Do I Get? 30 ciphers

What Am I Missing? More ciphers, also available for DOS!

How Much? $15 for registration and 200 additional puzzles, $26 for the Deluxe Edition, with a printed manual and case. $5 for each 200 puzzle pack after that.

How Do I Order? Nels Anderson, 92 Bishop Dr., Framingham, MA 01701-6515.

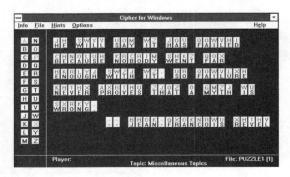

Nels Anderson's *Cipher for Windows* is a word game in which you attempt to discover the real meaning of an encrypted quotation or phrase. Each letter in the phrase has been replaced with another letter, and by determining which letters represent which, you begin to decipher the phrase. Simply pick a letter from the list on the left, and click the letter in the encryption box that you think it stands for. For instance, if you think "E" stands for "Y," click "E" on the left-hand list, and then any "Y" in the encrypted quote. Final score is based on the number of wrong guesses and the time it took to complete the puzzle.

There are a wealth of features in this program, including helps such as a total count of letter frequencies, a random "show letter" option that deciphers one at a time, a "clear wrong guesses" function that eliminates any wrong letters you may have entered, and a "show answer" box. Any puzzle can be accessed at any time. You can even create your own encryptions! Just enter the quote and it will encrypt it automatically. *Cipher for Windows*, also available in a DOS version, is a real bonanza for "crypt-o-quote" fans, and for a mere $15, you can hardly go wrong.

Millenium Auction

Who's it From? Eidolon

Where is It? X:\WINGAMES\
AUCTION\DEMO

How Do I Use It? Run DEMO.EXE in
Windows.

What Do I Get? Demo

How Much? $69.95

How Do I Order? Eidolon, 5716
Masholu Ave., Riverdale, NY 10471.

The hands-down winner for the single *oddest* title of the year goes to this little gem from the Bronx. That's right, a group of men with a vision set up shop under the name of Eidolon and, after two years, emerged with *Millenium Auction*. Vatche Kaladijan, a fresh-from-college techie, and Eric Roffmann, a mathematical physicist from Princeton, got together to create a game based on Roffmann's idea of a futuristic auction. Their team grew out of the New York art community, and was populated with people who were new to computers as an artistic medium and therefore brought no preconceptions to the project. The result is a game so unique that it seems as though it were developed in a bubble.

Millenium Auction has the feel of a board or party game, and the look of the finest CD-ROM games. The graphics design and modelling of the characters is simply beautiful, and a surreal atmosphere pervades the entire title. You begin by assuming the role of a wealthy art collector of the future. Each player has his or her own character dossier and a large supply of UN dollars.

This elite group enter the auction complex, where they mill about, gossip, and check out what's on the block today. Maybe it's a classic painting by Rubens, Pollock, Rembrandt, or some future artist. Maybe it's the sax Bill Clinton played on the Arsenio Hall Show, or a even a photo of J. Edgar Hoover in a dress. Each comes with a picture and description, and as an art collector you have to decide which will go up in value, which you might buy simply out of love, and which are forgeries.

You are helped in this quest by talking to the other art collectors, and even eavesdropping on their conversations. Each of these sequences is conveyed in strange montages and explosions of bizarre imagery. All of them are simply weird for the sake of being weird, but they add such a particular ambiance to the entire game that they become one of its most distinct features. Each of these conversations not only tells you what your colleagues feel about various objects up for auction, but also lets you in on the people and personal dramas of this art set. Various other resources, such as an old auction hand and several news sources, also help you in selecting objects to bid on. The bidding progresses in auction sequences that build to a fever pitch, but still manage to feel redundant after a time.

There are a wild range of art objects to choose from, with add-on sets promising still more. With such outstanding computer imaging and such a strange sensibility, as well as solid gameplay, *Millenium Auction* is one of the most surprising and distinct titles of the year.

David Leadbetter's Greens

Who's it From? MicroProse

Where is It? X:\DOSDEMO\GREENS

How Do I Use It? Type INSTALL at the DOS prompt.

What Do I Get? Demo

How Much? N/A

How Do I Order? MicroProse Entertainment Software, 180 Lakefront Dr., Hunt Valley, MD 21030-2245. (410) 771-1151.

It would take a crowbar and a blowtorch to pry my copy of *Links 386 Pro* away from me, but that doesn't mean I don't sometimes sneak around town with other golf programs. One of the more intriguing titles to come out of the computer golf boom was *David Leadbetter's Greens* from MicroProse.

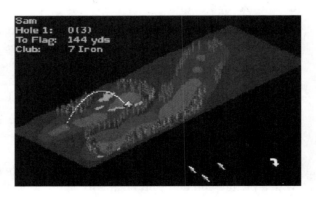

Greens was one of the first sports titles from MicroProse, as they began expanding beyond their traditional position as an industry-leader flight sim and strategy game maker. *Greens* was in the works when *Links* hit the market with its beautiful graphics. MicroProse fell back a bit and rethought *Greens* so that it would stand apart from *Links*. They added golf-instructor-to-the-pros David Leadbetter to the design team, and the result is a game with enough unique features to set it apart from the competition.

Greens' graphics are certainly less elaborate than those in *Links*, with a closer resemblance to MicroProse's flight worlds. What it adds, however, is Leadbetter himself, providing commentary on your game at various points, noting what you're doing wrong, and suggesting how to do it right. The base game comes with six different courses: Ballybrook, Buckland, Heath, Mountsummer Point, St. Augustine, Dunedin Country Club, and the Donald Ross Memorial Course, offering more variety than any of the competition. There are also a wide variety of game types, such as singles, threeball, fourball, bestball, threesomes, foursomes, tournaments, skins, and, even head-to-head with another player.

Play is very similar to other golf games, with a swing-meter operated by mouse clicks controlling swing strength and direction. What others don't offer, however, are *Greens* multiple viewing angles, so you can watch your shots as never before. Altogether, there are enough new features to keep *Greens* fresh and different, setting it apart from *Links* and the other golf games on the market. It has its own merits, and is worth a look.

Ultimate NFL Coaches Club Football

Who's it From? MicroProse

Where is It? X:\DOSDEMO\FOOTBALL

How Do I Use It? Type FOOTBALL at the DOS prompt.

What Do I Get? Demo

How Much? $57.95

How Do I Order? MicroProse Entertainment Software, 180 Lakefront Dr., Hunt Valley, MD 21030-2245, (410) 771-1151.

Never let it be said that MicroProse is afraid to go toe-to-toe with some prestigious competition. In *Greens*, they took on the landmark *Links* golf game, and with *NFL Coaches Club Football*, they went up against Dynamix's superb *Front Page Sports: Football*. Now they've pushed *Coaches Club* even further with their newly enhanced *Ultimate NFL Coaches Club Football CD-ROM*. How does it fare against its prestigious competition? Pretty damn well, it turns out.

Coaches Club Football has many of the elements of traditional football games, such as single game or season play, multiple views, play calling, and so on. There are full 3-D views of the action on the gridiron, and from various other locations. (There's even an instant replay option, and these can be saved for later viewing.) Hundreds of real NFL plays are also available, and, you can even control key players in the action. You can choose and change formations, call audibles, even design your own plays. Even better: there's full modem support, so you can go head-to-head with a friend!

Since this is a licensed title, your competition is the other NFL teams based on their actual strengths, weaknesses, and unique coaching strategies. All the plays in professional football are here to play against, complete with team names, team logos, team colors, and the actual player names and stats from the 1993 season. NFL players and coaches have contributed their input to *Coaches Club Football*, so that unique strategies and player profiles add to the realism. All the options you could possibly want in a football title are here, from trading to full stats and realistic modelling of results. The graphics and sound effects are quite sharp: some of the best in any sports game yet. All in all, this is a solid title that adds a new player to the computer gridiron.

Front Page Sports: Baseball

Who's it From? Sierra On-Line/ Dynamix

Where is It? X:\DOSDEMO\ BASEBALL

How Do I Use It? Type SHOW or SIM at the DOS prompt.

What Do I Get? Demo

How Much? $54.95

How Do I Order? Sierra On-Line, P.O. Box 53250, Bellevue, WA 98015-3250. (800) 757-7707.

Who cares if the baseball players stay on strike next year? They were a bunch of over-paid underwear models anyway. Besides, *Front Page Sports: Baseball* puts an entire season inside your PC with such realism, accuracy, and control that you won't even mind if the strike continues or not.

Dynamix's follow-up to their award-winning *Front Page Sports: Football* is every bit as detailed and challenging. Every feature you could possibly want is here: real Major League Players and their statistics; nine different stadiums, each authentically modelled; season scheduling; trading; exhaustive statistical reports on every element of play; injuries; real-world physics; and top-flight graphics and sound effects. One season rolls over to the next; players age, are injured, become better (or worse), and retire; you can scout schools for talent and build your own franchise, then develop players in the Minor League before bringing them into the Majors.

Graphics and gameplay are more realistic than anything that has been seen in any baseball game before. Animations, particularly the players themselves, are sharp and detailed. Computer opponents certainly seem formidable enough, with coaches and players offering a fair challenge. The initial release sported some pesky statistical bugs, but that should be fixed by the time you read this.

Front Page Sports continues a solid, industry-defining tradition of sports sims with another great title. We can sit back and enjoy *Baseball* as we eagerly wait for hockey, soccer, and basketball to make their way to the Front Page.

THREE

ROLE-PLAYING
&
ADVENTURE GAMES

When role-playing games came into their own in the 1970s with Gary Gygax's *Dungeons and Dragons*, some saw them as a playground for the imagination, others merely as escapist nonsense. What the critics failed to see was that, once freed from the bombast of media images, people—mostly young—were able to get together and create whole worlds which existed only in their own minds. They were turning away from the passivity of television and turning toward the activity of creation. Granted, much of this creation involved endless quests, swordplay, and teenage male fantasy set against landscapes right out of J.R.R. Tolkien or Robert E. Howard. Role-playing gave a good number of outsiders and class losers a place where they belonged, as well as giving a good number of psychos something new to be obsessed with other than Jodie Foster. The Christian Right saw role-playing as a kind of neo-Satanism, and everyone got worked into a perfect tizzy either defending or criticizing it.

When it all died down, we were left with what we started with: games. More than that, they were games without a board or playing pieces...games that didn't require quarters, a joystick, or a video screen. As one could have expected, however, role-playing games became one of the earliest kind of games brought to computer, thereby rendering the completely imaginary completely literal.

Initially the games were short on graphics, offering either text descriptions or crude graphics. The first to make a big splash was *Wizardry* by a small East Coast company called Sir-Tech. Using simple line renditions of dungeons, *Wizardry* gave

ROLE-PLAYING AND ADVENTURE GAMES

A *role-playing game*, or *RPG*, is usually a quest, often a fantasy quest, involving a character or a party of characters under the user's control. These characters traverse a landscape, talk to people they meet, collect objects, and fight. They have *hit points* that diminish when they are injured and need to be increased, or the character dies. RPG characters usually progress through *levels* or *ranks* as they gain experience. The emphasis is on combat and magic.

An *adventure game* also puts the user in control of characters, but these characters remain consistent, and do *not* have hit points or progress through levels. This type of game is dialog driven and usually involves puzzle solving and character interaction. The puzzles generally center around collecting objects and using them at the proper time to overcome an obstacle.

computer gamers their first real taste of a "dungeon-crawl," in which a party of characters took part in a fantasy quest. Standard role-playing skills and numerical values (strength, dexterity, etc.), spell-casting, and weapons recreated the familiar trappings of fantasy role-playing games in a visual environment. Along with Origin's *Ultima* series, *Wizardry* began slowly pushing the genre forward, with slightly better graphics, more story, and more adventure. Soon, there were as many varieties of role-playing games as there were strategy games, and people kept returning to them, looking for adventure and a little fantasy.

At the same time, straight adventure games were also coming of age. Sierra On-Line's adventures became hugely popular series: the *King's Quest*, *Police Quest*, *Quest for Glory*, and *Leisure Suit Larry* series have all lasted game after game, with each new game featuring new technology and a further refinement of the Sierra style. Using an icon that changed functions as the user pressed the right mouse button, the Sierra games boiled interacting with an environment down to a simple series of commands: walk, talk, pickup, use, and so on.

LucasArts was also working hard on *their* engine, which used an icon bar for commands. The adventure game soon was omnipresent, reaching probably the broadest base of users simply because it has the broadest base of appeal. Adventure games also have the largest range of styles and approaches: from dark and horrific, to funny, to mysterious to, well, adventurous. They allow users to get into a story and characters with a minimum of fuss, without having to worry about hit points, combat, or game manuals. Because so many types of game can be labelled "adventure," they will probably continue to be the largest category with the most mass appeal.

☆ System Shock ☆

Who's It From? Origin Systems, developed by Looking Glass

Where Is It? X:\DOSDEMO\SSHOCK

How Do I Use It? Type SSHOCK at the DOS prompt.

What Do I Get? Interactive demo.

How Much? $79.95

How Do I Order? Origin Systems, 12940 Research Blvd., Austin, TX 78750. (800) 245-4525.

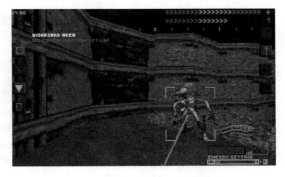

It is 2072. Something has happened in the Citadel, a high-tech orbital research facility. The SHODAN computer security system has malfunctioned almost since its installation. First, scientists are infected with a viral mutation agent (mutagen), apparently due to faulty computer software. Robots and computer systems inexplicably go haywire. Infected researchers begin showing psychopathic tendencies, and start dying. Riots erupt throughout the base. When a military transport is sent to sort things out, the space station's defense weapons destroy it. A short time later, SHODAN announces its intention to control all life aboard the Citadel. Robots take over the station and start slaughtering the human inhabitants. A brief message from some survivors warns that Earth is in danger from SHODAN, then all contact stops. The massacre appears complete.

But in its attempt to eradicate all human life on the Citadel, SHODAN has missed one person.

It all began when you tried to hack into the Citadel's computers. When you were discovered, corrupt vice-president Edward Diego offered you an alternative to going to jail: hack him into SHODAN and get a neural implant in exchange. You keep up your part of the bargain, and he keeps his. For the last six months you have been in a healing coma on the Citadel, recovering from the neural implant surgery. You awake in the base hospital to find the base a scene of carnage. The implant provides you with a view enhanced by bio-monitors, multifunction displays, energy and health indicators, and numerous attachments that allow you to jack into cyberspace, map the base, auto-read electronic messages

SYSTEM SHOCK: **LEVEL ONE**

You have one mission in *System Shock:* destroy the evil computer SHODAN before it destroys you. In the course of your quest you will come across a heap of weapons, some better than others, and face numerous obstacles. Two things primarily bar your way: security systems and bad guys.

- First things first. Explore the entire med lab, especially the trap doors and closets. You'll find the log entries, including one of your own listing all the information about the Citadel that you know (including doorway access codes). Gather up all this stuff and keep it. There is also a metal bar lying on the floor. Since this will be your only weapon until you find the dart gun and the mag pistol, pick it up and keep it in hand.

-  You gotta clean out the bad guys before you can start destroying security (by taking out the security cameras). In the beginning, you'll face the mutants in quantity. These were once poor saps who thought they could get a good-paying job on a space station, and wound up the subject of bizarre experiments gone awry. They tend to gurgle a bit, which makes it easier to locate them aurally, but visually they can be hard to find, as they stay to the shadows and don't leap out until the last moment. At first, all you have is the metal bar, but a few whacks from this will cave their heads in good.

- Pick up and read *all* e-mail and log entries. They contain crucial information, including security codes.

- When you find the dart gun (just outside of the surgery suite), start using that on the mutants and even the cyborgs. There are darts to be found all over, and they come in two varieties: needle darts just drug the buggers, while the others have tips that explode on impact. Two exploding darts should take out a mutant, and three will work on cyborgs.

- Search everyone, even the mutants. Ammo, health patches, and a lot of other useful objects can be found in abundance on corpses.

- When you get to the far side of Level One (where the hopping security robot will kill you a few times), look for a blue plate set in the floor. Step on this plate to travel to a lower-level viewing station. Look for a switch along the bottom of the wall and throw it. This activates the plate at the center of the room. Step on it and it will lift you up to a kind of viewing alcove. Solve the puzzle by clicking the Xs and dashes to complete the circuit, and the force door will unlock. If you're playing with puzzles on, it's the only way to continue.

- Past the force door you find a kind of storage area and clinic for cyborgs. In one of these rooms there is a tiny alcove with a human outline on the wall. This converts people into cyborgs when they die. Throw the switch, and it turns off the cyborg conversion and reconfigures the station for healing purposes. Now, if you die, you'll be brought back to life, instead of turned into a cyborg.

- Kill all the cyborgs in "storage" before they activate, then build up health levels and take out the big guy on the platform (it ain't easy). Make your way to the banks of computers and toss a grenade into the room. Once these computers are destroyed, SHODAN will be very, *very* pissed, and cyborgs will start coming out of the walls. Try using grenades on them, but in all likelihood they'll kill you, you'll come back to life in the cyborg conversion chamber, and simply make your way to the exit (just past this chamber).

- Be ready for a surprise when you take the elevator (complete with elevator music) down to Level Two. Mutants a-go-go!

View angle　　Posture control　　Health indicator

Bio-monitors

Full-screen mode

360° view

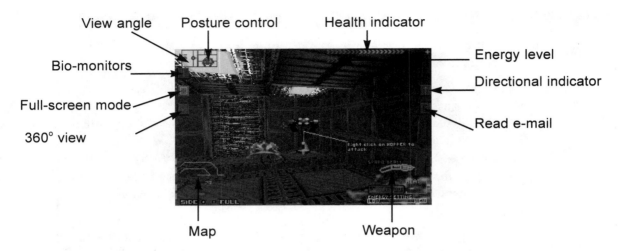

Energy level

Directional indicator

Read e-mail

Map　　　　　　　　　Weapon

and logs, and generally start kicking ass and taking down names. As you go along you find other attachments, some giving you a 360° view of your surroundings, others enhancing your vision, and so on.

Welcome to *System Shock:* there has never been anything like it. It is a complete evocation of a hellish future world, where you are part human and part machine. You are the only person left on the Citadel, and you must hunt and kill the mutants and robots, disable SHODAN's security, and unravel its plans and secrets. At first all you have to protect yourself with is a metal bar, but you soon pick up all manner of high-tech weapons. Slowly, you piece together the final days and hours of the Citadel by reading the e-mail of the last survivors. In order to progress through the eight levels of the Citadel, you have to get past secured doors by solving puzzles, kill almost anything that moves, pick up more neural enhancements, and, most unique of all, explore cyberspace.

On each level, you can jack into the computers and explore SHODAN's world. Unlike the 3D texture maps of the rest of the game, the Cyberspace sequences are composed of polygons, resembling nothing so much as Spectre VR. Once you're in, you have a limited amount of time to explore, pick up useful software, throw switches to unlock doors in the "real world," and generally harass SHODAN and thwart its plans. If you spend too much time inside cyberspace, SHODAN will track you down and eject you. Forcibly. And painfully.

System Shock smokes. It is the most fully immersive game world I have ever experienced. Not since Looking Glass's last big hits, the *Ultima Underworld* games, have I felt this *inside* a virtual world. Controls allow you to move in any direction at a variety of speeds. You can jump, crouch, crawl on your stomach, look all the way up or down, and lean to either side. And these are more than gimmicks: certain places can only be reached by crawling on your belly, and you can use a wall for cover while you lean to one side and fire on an enemy. Monitors track your health, vital signs, and power levels, and new and more complex enhancements can be plugged into your neural implant to help you in your quest. The graphics, though often dark, are beautifully rendered and feature a wide range of locations and creatures. Every level is full of rooms, hidden passageways, and tight places to discover and explore. Mutants charge out of the shadows, assassin robots quietly stalk through the corridors, security drones hide around every corner. And hovering above it all is the godlike, Gigeresque presence of SHODAN. SHODAN ignores you at first, but when you destroy a crucial security station, it begins stalking you in earnest, and its rage knows no bounds.

The atmosphere is thick with danger and despair. You pick up logs and e-mails from the last survivors, who made a valiant and tragic stand against SHODAN. Their final messages are scrawled in blood on the walls, and their mutilated corpses litter the floors. Weapons, ammo, health packs, grenades, mines, and all manner of objects can be found on each of the eight levels. You have to solve puzzles to get through certain doors, and slowly chip away at SHODAN's security systems in order to erode its iron grip on the station.

There are so many unique and entertaining aspects of *System Shock* that it's hard to know where to begin. The game world is stark and fully developed, and the story consistently intrigues. Sound effects are dense and effective, and the pounding, ominous music provides just the right atmosphere, particularly on a Gravis Ultrasound board, which is fully, and effectively, supported. Numerous configuration settings mean you can set the game for as much or as little combat as you desire, make the story more elaborate, or increase the difficulty of puzzles. There are so many options that no matter what kind of game you're looking for, you'll find something in *System Shock* to delight. This is an exciting, entertaining, wholly unique game, so fully realized in all its diverse aspects, and so completely immersive, that it raises computer gaming to a new level.

☆ Ultima Underworld ☆

Who's It From? Origin Systems, developed by Looking Glass

Where Is It? X:\DOSDEMO\UW

How Do I Use It? Copy to hard drive and type UWCONFIG at the DOS prompt.

What Do I Get? Interactive demo.

How Much? $49.95 for both *Underworld*s on one CD-ROM.

How Do I Order? Origin Systems, 12940 Research Blvd., Austin, TX 78750. (800) 245-4525.

As if it weren't enough that Origin created one of the landmark role-playing games of all time in *Ultima*, they went on to make even their *spin-offs* from *Ultima* computer gaming landmarks. When it was released, *Ultima Underworld: The Stygian Abyss* was one of the most revolutionary game engines anybody had seen. It wasn't just that it moved the *Ultima* series from a top-down to a first-person game, which was nothing new, but that it offered the first "true" 3D perspective. Its smooth-flowing animation was completely unlike the step-by-step perspective of other games. The view moved and scrolled just as the human view would. What's more, you could look up and down: something that had never been done before. It launched an entire new generation of role-playing games, and still holds up despite the intervening years. *Ultima Underworld: The Stygian Abyss* finds the Avatar facing danger yet again. It appears that Lord British has assigned Baron Almric to lead an experimental settlement on the Isle of the Avatar. Unfortunately, it's placed right over the Stygian Abyss. After being summoned to the Isle by a ghostly presence, the Avatar is accused of kidnapping the Baron's daughter, forcing him to travel deep into the Abyss to rescue her and prove his virtue. But darker things are afoot, and the Avatar has to thwart the Guardian's evil plot to destroy Brittania.

Ultima Underworld features combat almost to the exclusion of all else, with monsters seemingly lurking around each corner. Oh, there are some puzzles and people to speak with, but the story is thin and the emphasis is on exploring the dark and foreboding underworld, and defeating its creatures. One of the most unique elements of *Underworld* is its magic system, which requires the user to collect ruinstones from various levels of the abyss. Each spell is composed of several ruins, and cast by arranging the ruins in the proper order. There's also a detailed automapping feature, which allows players to actually jot reminder notes right on the map.

Ultima Underworld was a huge success, which meant, of course, that it was followed by a sequel. *Ultima Underworld II: The Labyrinth of Worlds* improved upon the original, fixed its weakness of content and added exciting new twists.

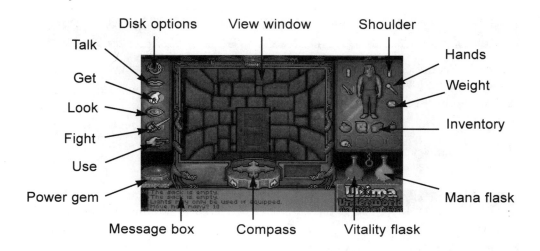

Talk — Disk options — View window — Shoulder

Hands

Get

Look

Weight

Fight

Inventory

Use

Power gem

Mana flask

Message box — Compass — Vitality flask

While the original *Ultima Underworld* was carried by its graphics and action, the second takes these elements, improves them, and goes even further. The story finds the Avatar and Lord British celebrating his victories over the evil Guardian. Suddenly, the festivities are interrupted by darkening skies: the Guardian has encased the castle within a large black gem, trapping everyone inside while his evil allies plunder the land. Determined to break the evil spell that binds the castle, the Avatar journeys into the monster-inhabited lower levels. There, he finds black gems which enable him to travel between several worlds, and only by conquering each world and breaking the Guardian's hold upon it, can the Avatar save Brittania.

Underworld II features more depth, more problem solving, and more character interaction than the original. One of its most striking features is the design of the numerous worlds with distinct looks and characteristics. There are worlds of ice, worlds of fire, and so on, each with unique problems: without the proper spells and equipment, the Avatar slips and slides in the ice world, and burns to death in the fire world. The graphics resolution seems altogether higher and more detailed than the first *Underworld*, and more attention has been paid to sound this time around.

These games are now available together on one CD-ROM from Origin, making for a great value and another required element of any role-playing game collection.

Shadowcaster

Who's It From? Origin Systems, developed by Raven Software

Where Is It? X:\DOSDEMO\ SHADOW

How Do I Use It? Copy to hard drive and type SHADOW at the DOS prompt.

What Do I Get? Interactive demo.

How Much? $39.95 on disk, $69.95 on CD-ROM.

How Do I Order? Origin Systems, 12940 Research Blvd., Austin, TX 78750. (800) 245-4525.

As we can see by some of the other titles covered so far, this has been a renaissance year for role-playing games, with some of the best titles we've seen in quite some time. One of the debuts which made it even more impressive was that of Raven Software, who put some new wrinkles in traditional role-playing design and delivered an exceptional title called *Shadowcaster*. (Raven, of course, has since gone on to do *CyClones* and *Heretic*.) This is one of the few RPGs that I stuck with straight through to the end, no matter what other titles were vying for my attention.

Shadowcaster's story centers around your character, Kirt. As the game opens, Kirt has been spirited away from his land to protect him from the ravages of a civil war, fought between The People and those who worship the evil god Malkor. Evil is driven away, but The People lose all they had, including, in time, their special power. They long had the ability to metamorphose into other creatures, assuming not only their shape but their powers as well. As time went on, only two remained who had the power to morph, and to these two was born a child, Kirt. To protect the infant from the encroaching evil of of the dark lord Veste, they send him away to grow to maturity in the safety of a foreign land. Now the time has come for Kirt to assume his birthright as Shadowcaster, returning to his people to defeat Veste.

The game places you in this land with little to protect yourself but your wits and skills. As you travel ever-further, you gain the ability to become new creatures by finding special obelisks, and grow stronger for the final confrontation with Veste. You can wield magic, fight, and morph for short periods of time into whatever monster is best suited to the task. One level, for example, takes place entirely underwater, where only the frog-like Kapha can survive. If you're severely wounded,

ORIGIN KEEPS PUSHING THE ENVELOPE

Origin Systems has always been on the cutting edge of interactive entertainment. From their *Wing Commander* games, to *Ultima, Ultima Underworld,* and now *System Shock* and *Bioforge,* they have consistently pushed the envelope more than any other company. This year proved yet again that this Texas giant is one of the most innovative gaming companies around.

The success of *System Shock* is the direct result of the smooth-flowing, immersive environments first created by Looking Glass for the *Ultima Underworld* series. Raven's *Shadowcaster* also took Origin in new directions this year with a unique, completely enjoyable spin on *Underworld,* and proved Origin still has the ability to surprise their customers with new designs and approaches.

The *Ultima* series reached near-perfection in its multi-part *Ultima VII,* but, true to Origin's intent to reinvent the series every few years, they took *Ultima VIII: Pagan* in a completely different direction than its predecessor. A change in the viewing angle was the least of the alterations. The Avatar, always accompanied by his trusty friends, is now solo, and his face is completely obscured throughout the game by a large helmet, making him look a bit like a robot. The game is much darker in tone, and the Avatar, who once stressed various virtues, is called upon in numerous instances to break each one of these virtues, committing thefts, sacrifices, and murders. Quite a few gamers were put off not only by these changes, but by the introduction of arcade sequences—anathema to most role-playing gamers. On the whole, however, *Pagan* was criticized all out of proportion to its quality: it was a new riff on an old chestnut, and provided a fresh change of pace and some new challenges.

The speed bumps Origin hit with *Pagan,* however, only got bigger with *Pacific Strike,* which shipped with so many problems and was received with such disdain that Origin felt compelled to apologize for it. It was only a momentary downturn, however, and they came back stronger than ever with two of the hottest titles of the year: *Wing Commander Armada* (introducing both strategic *and* modem play to the *WC* world) and *System Shock* (see above). With *Wing of Glory* (a World War I flyer), *Bioforge* (an "interactive move"), and the ultra-hot, star-studded *Wing Commander III* due out before year-end, what started out as a rocky year for computer gaming's most ambitious company may end up their best year ever.

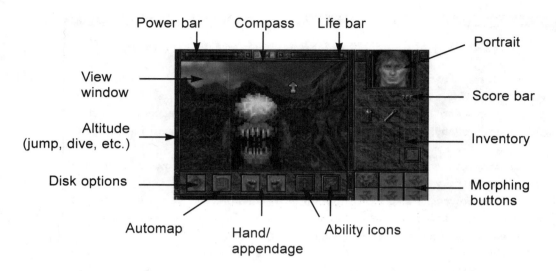

Power bar Compass Life bar

Portrait

View window

Score bar

Altitude (jump, dive, etc.)

Inventory

Disk options

Morphing buttons

Automap   Hand/appendage   Ability icons

you can turn into one of the diminutive Caun, which heal at a faster rate than other creatures.

Developed using a highly modified version of the *Wolfenstein 3D* engine, *Shadowcaster* features sharp, smooth-scrolling graphics and an eye-catching look. The interface allows you to switch between combat, magic, and morphing with ease, and, as you assume the ability to become more creatures, you gain the ability to use new powers. The eye-ball-like Opsis, for example, can throw cold blasts and missiles at enemies, and even have a lethal death-blast. The mountainous Grost are impervious to attack and fire, and can create earthquakes by stomping their feet. Each obstacle, enemy, or puzzle you come across requires a subtly different use of one of your creatures' powers, adding extra dimensions of challenge to the game.

Shadowcaster comes in both a floppy version and an enhanced CD-ROM, featuring a new level and animated cut scenes.

The Elder Scrolls 1: Arena

Who's It From? Bethesda Softworks
Where Is It? X:\DOSDEMO\ARENA
How Do I Use It? Type ARENA at the DOS prompt.

What Do I Get? Interactive demo
How Much? $69.95
How Do I Order? Bethesda Softworks, 1370 Picard Dr., Rockville, MD 20850.

One of the newcomers to the world of role-playing games this year was Bethesda Softworks, best known for their *Terminator* games. The first title in *The Elder Scrolls* series, *Arena*, is a single-player adventure solidly in the tradition of *Underworld*, but with a good execution and enough unique elements to make it one of the more talked-about games of late.

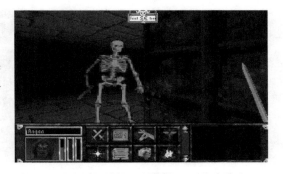

The adventure begins with the Emperor's wizard, Jager Tharn, turning traitor and using the Staff of Chaos to blast the Emperor into another dimension. He shatters the staff and flings its pieces around the world, then kills a sorceress friend of yours and throws you in the dungeon as a likely threat to his schemes. As the game begins, your friend, who is clinging to this world in a more ethereal form, releases you from the dungeon. You begin your quest to find the pieces of the Staff of Chaos, kill Tharn, and free the Emperor.

While the *Underworld* games are limited to dungeons, as their titles imply, *Arena* breaks free from this and allows you to explore entire towns and their surroundings. As you traverse this extensive world, you perform numerous subquests in order to find enough clues to continue your quest. Non-player character (referred to as "NPCs" by gamers) interaction is fairly extensive, and by talking to the various characters, and performing deeds for them, you pick up information necessary to continue with the story. There are doors which can only be opened by solving riddles, and dangerous foes to battle throughout the world. While the graphics aren't quite as good as those in *Underworld*, an effective bag of sound effects more than make up for this. A large selection of character classes (including knights, assassins, and so forth), an inventive spell-casting engine, and a generally inspired design and execution make *Arena* a standout title in the world of role-playing games.

The Elder Scrolls: Arena, originally released as a floppy title, is now available on CD-ROM, featuring recorded dialog and added animations.

Menzoberranzan

Who's It From? Developed by DreamForge, released by SSI.

Where Is It? X:\DOSDEMO\MENDEMO

How Do I Use It? Copy to hard drive and type MENZO at the DOS prompt.

What Do I Get? Noninteractive demo

How Much? $80.00

How Do I Order? SSI, 675 Almanor Ave., Ste. 201, Sunnyvale, CA 94086-2901. (800) 245-4525.

DreamForge has been doing some truly top-flight program work for SSI lately, and with what is likely the last SSI Advanced Dungeons & Dragons title, they've really thrown their hat over the windmill. *Menzoberranzan* may well be the best AD&D title yet, featuring inspired graphics, an involved storyline, and an intuitive interface. It flies in the face of SSI's TSR-imposed limits (more action and less story), to deliver a complex world, involved political machinations, and interesting characters.

Menzoberranzan is based on R.A. Salvatore's novel *The Legacy*, which explores the mysterious culture of the Drow. A race of nocturnal, subterranean, dark-skinned elves, the Drow are known for their sadism and their worship of dark creatures. Unwary surface dwellers in the Forgotten Realms are often snatched by the Drow, and nobody has been able to stop them. One night, as your group of companions celebrates a recent victory in Icewind Dale, a Drow raiding party strikes. They raze the town and kill any who try to oppose them, dragging dozens of innocent citizens off to their underground lair. The villagers immediately turn on a kindly Drow named Drizzt, blaming him for the raid. Though uninvolved, Drizzt is determined to set right the evil his people have perpetrated, and agrees to lead your party to the mysterious Drow town of Menzoberranzan to rescue the kidnapped villagers.

As you journey deep into dark and evil lands, you learn more about the complex culture of the Drow, solve puzzles, and, of course, fight. Along the way you become involved in the politics of the Drow, who are controlled by a series of noble Houses, all vying for more political power. As you're forced to help some

Houses defeat others, you begin to upset the balance of power, possibly enabling one House to unleash an ultimate destruction upon the world. Refreshingly, the emphasis in *Menzoberranzan* seems to be on story and character interaction, weaving a complex tale of people and power that goes beyond the traditional hack-and-slash game.

This is not to say there is no combat: an entire bevy of new monsters haunt the darkened lands you must traverse, and new weapons, spells, and prayers are available to help you defeat them. Combat is effected using a simple, real-time engine that brings a fight to a speedy resolution. The first-person perspective and lush graphics give you a front-row view of some hair-raising critters as they either kill you or suffer a gruesome death. Add an extensive soundtrack, elaborate cut scenes, countless sound effects, and spoken dialog, and you have one of the most complete and fulfilling role-playing games this line has ever produced. It's certainly one of the most involving and best produced I've seen so far this year.

Dark Legions

Who's It From? Developed by Silicon Knights, released by SSI.

Where Is It? X:\DOSDEMO\ DARKLEG

How Do I Use It? Type DLEGIONS at the DOS prompt.

What Do I Get? DOS demo of commercial release.

How Much? $60.00 (disk); $45.00 (CD-ROM)

How Do I Order? SSI, 675 Almanor Ave., Ste. 201, Sunnyvale, CA 94086-2901. (800) 245-4525.

As a chess-like strategy game in which the combatants actually fight, *Dark Legions* owes a debt to *Archon*, and, to a lesser degree, *Battle Chess*. Neither of those notable games, however, were as entertaining, well-designed, or engrossing as Silicon Knight's follow-up to *Fantasy Empires*. This is one of the best fantasy-strategy games to come down the pike in a long, long time.

The premise has you using creatures from a world called Tahr Carog to fight battles against your opponent for control of the universe. The games are played

THE MONSTERS OF DARK LEGIONS

Vampires

A very *dangerous*, flying bloodsucker, the vampire siphons off life-force and turns all but undead creatures into zombies under their control! Nasty critters.

Fire Elementals

These seem to be one of the best "light infantry" in the game: agile and well-armed, with a "Supernova" suicide attack that torches anyone within several squares. Water elementals have their number, however.

Demons

Moving fortresses of power, with a six-space "Scream of Terror," you'll want a demon around for any serious brawl. Their power makes them good orb-holders.

Seer

Well-nigh useless in battle, but essential for finding traps and illusionary or invisible characters.

across varying landscapes overlaid with a chess-like grid to regulate movement, as you and your foe jockey your warriors into position. Both players have an Orb of Power, which is given to one of their warriors before the game begins. This Orb becomes a de facto king, and the goal is to nab the other player's Orb before he or she gets yours.

None of this really hints at the depth built into this game. To begin with, there are options galore, allowing for a lot of replayability. In starting a new game, you can either choose Quick Start, which offers a number of predesigned games of

Conjurers

Expensive and frail, but worth it, the conjurer can create other creatures to send into battle.

Berserkers

The cheapest "shock troops." The same goes for Orcs, though Orcs have poor revitalization. Treat them like pawns and use 'em to wear the opponent down.

Templar

Pitiful in combat, but necessary for healing and revitalization.

Phantom

Though these undead creatures are slow, they are also invisible and have a vicious attack that *permanently* reduces a victim's ability to regain stamina. Another good candidate for orb-holder.

varying lengths and complexity, or Setup to make your own. Settings allow for human versus human (side-by-side at the keyboard or over modem), or human versus the computer AI, which can be set from "Brain Dead" to "Merciless." Brain Dead is not only stupid, but hesitates in combat, while Merciless has double your credits and a jacked-up artificial intelligence. You can give yourself more credits to buy a bigger army and other aids, or less for more of a challenge. Once these specifications are chosen, you can buy units, traps, and magical rings and plan your strategy.

Dark Legions has taken an old idea and given it new life in this truly engaging game, with superb production and design and virtually limitless depth of play. There are real challenges here, and attentive players will try different formations and combinations of creatures, manipulating special powers, rings, and traps, and finding new ways of using the landscape for a long time to come.

Ravenloft

Who's It From? Developed by DreamForge, released by SSI.

Where Is It? X:\DOSDEMO\RLOFT

How Do I Use It? Type RLOFT at the DOS prompt.

What Do I Get? Interactive demo

How Much? $80.00 (disc); $65.00 (CD-ROM).

How Do I Order? SSI, 675 Almanor Ave., Ste. 201, Sunnyvale, CA 94086-2901. (800) 245-4525.

Ravenloft: Strahd's Possession is a fresh departure for SSI, bringing TSR's popular "Ravenloft" paper role-playing game to computer for the first time. "Ravenloft," the horror side of TSR's fantasy lines, has also been turned into a successful series of novels. Concentrating on more traditional horror monsters, such as vampires, zombies, ghouls, bats, and were-creatures, these games seek to build an atmosphere of dread rather than one of fantasy.

Ravenloft begins with only two people in your party, though two more NPCs can join in the course of the game. It will take you through the dangerous lands of Ravenloft, ruled by the iron hand of Lord Strahd, and populated by both creatures of the night and innocents just trying to survive. Strahd is a vampire lord, banished to the region called Borovia, where he rules Ravenloft. Reminiscent of Kairn, the evil vampiric ruler from DreamForge's *Veil of Darkness*, Strahd is a brooding, lurking presence throughout the game. Unlucky travelers have been hung on pikes throughout the land, Strahd's grim warnings nailed to their skeletal chests. Unfortunately, Strahd is the key to finding Lord Behlt's holy symbol, which he believes is the Holy Symbol of Ravenkind, a source of great power. In

TO D&D, OR NOT TO D&D: SSI DROPS TSR

In the early Eighties, with the rights to create computer versions of TSR's Advanced Dungeons & Dragons game rules (the granddaddy of role-playing games) under their belts, SSI created a number of AD&D fantasy series, such as *Forgotten Realms, Eye of the Beholder*, the "Gold Box" games, and others. The AD&D name and familiarity served SSI well through the entire computer gaming boom of the 1980s and a bit into the 90s, with strong sales and new titles released on a regular basis.

Due to the limitations of the AD&D rules, however, SSI's role-playing games began getting repetitious and overly familiar. This past year, SSI released a terrific series of D&D and AD&D products looking to break that cycle. Titles such as *Stronghold* and *Fantasy Empires*, with their strategic warfare and kingdom building element; the "dungeon creator" programs *Dungeon Hack* and *Unlimited Adventures*; *Menzoberranzan* and the 3DO game *Slayer*; and the horror world of *Ravenloft* injected some new life into the steadily flagging TSR license, but only enough life for a last gasp. Their long-awaited new AD&D engine for the *Dark Sun* game ran months behind schedule and wildly over budget, and when finished, would only last for two modestly successful games: *Shattered Lands* and *Wake of the Ravager*. Early in the year, SSI announced that 1994 would mark the last year of their TSR license, ending one of the longest-running series of related games in computer gaming history.

A number of factors were behind this divorce, but one can clearly see that TSR had outstayed their welcome. Grumbles about their iron-fisted control of project content and desire to keep the games primarily combat-based (and not story-driven) had surrounded the *Ravenloft* project, among others, and *Dark Sun* wound up a developmental nightmare. Where there was room to do something different, SSI was often forced to do the same old thing, over and over again. At the same time, SSI's non-TSR games were looking quite handsome, and it became evident that the narrow constraints of the AD&D rules were more hindrance than help. With the help of a series of development teams, such as Silicon Knights, Raven, DreamForge, and their in-house projects team, SSI was turning out a large number of high-quality products. *Veil of Darkness, Dark Legions, CyClones, The Summoning*, and *Flashback* proved that, freed from AD&D, SSI and their teams could spread their wings a little more. Of course, you can also probably cite the flagging value of the AD&D games, since if they were still profitable, "creative differences" or not, SSI would likely have kept doing them.

Now SSI can turn to new and more inventive worlds, and from the looks of some of their new and forthcoming titles, they will be some of the most enjoyable worlds this company has ever created.

order to find the symbol, you first must learn about Strahd and what he wants. At first, he regards your party as merely a nuisance, sending out the gypsy race known as the Vistani to capture the symbol and deal with you. As you get further, he begins to toy with you, but soon learns that this small band of adventurers is more of a threat than he first realized.

Ravenloft features a large world and a whole new batch of monsters and spells. The first-person perspective for your party of four is quite ably handled, and in some respects, is better than *Underworld*. All dialog is spoken throughout, and the voice-overs add depth to the various characters—good and bad—that you meet along the way. Most impressive are the extensive cut scenes, many running at least ten megs, with the finale weighing in at fifty-five megs! Needless to say, both voice-overs and most cut scenes are not in the non-CD-ROM version of *Ravenloft*. In terms of graphics, cinematics, story, and sound effects, this is an ambitious and satisfying endeavor.

☆ Alone in the Dark 1 & 2 ☆

Who's It From? I-Motion/Interplay

Where Is It? X:\DOSDEMO\ ALONE1 & ALONE2

How Do I Use It? Type ALONE (Alone 1) or INSTALL (Alone 2) at the DOS prompt. To run Alone 2 once installed, type TATOU.

How Much? $59.95

How Do I Order? Interplay Productions, 17922 Fitch Ave., Irvine, CA 92714. (800) INTERPLAY.

The two *Alone in the Dark* games are the most distinctive, satisfying, and downright *bizarre* games in a long time. Their polygonal graphics pack a mean punch that you won't get in other, more traditional horror games.

In the first *Alone in the Dark*, you play Edward Carnby, a private detective who gets a job inventorying a generic, spooky old house whose owner has recently been driven mad. When a demon dog and a zombie attack you within the first two minutes of the game, it doesn't take long to figure out that you've got a long night ahead of you. Your only goal is to escape the house alive.

ALONE IN THE DARK TIPS

You'll probably find the control of *AITD* tricky at first—but with some practice, you'll be able to down those ghouls with more finesse than Ash from *The Evil Dead* ever could. Here are some tips for the first game.

- In the attic, make sure the first thing you do is push the dresser in front of the window. This will prevent the demon dog from getting in!

- Your second precaution should be to push the trunk over the trapdoor, preventing the zombie from popping up and surprising you.

- Always position yourself around a corner in combat. This will make zombies and other nasties less likely to hit you.

- With most edged weapons, the slash attack is the most effective, being the fastest and leaving a smaller window of attack for your opponent.

Any resemblance to other, more conventional horror games stops here: *AITD*'s new graphic techniques make for a unique, immensely enjoyable, and original playing experience. First of all, the characters in the game are polygonal. While the polygonal look is peculiar, the characters move with fluidity and realism. Second, instead of a scrolling screen, the game uses different camera angles. As you walk through a door or to a different part of a room, the screen switches to a new perspective. Although some of these angles can be irritating when you're in combat (it can be damn near impossible to see who's doing what to whom), it adds to the interactive-movie-like environment of *AITD*. Finally, there is no graphic frame: the entire game is presented full-screen. When you press the Enter key, an options menu pops up, letting you open, search, jump, or use inventory objects.

Suffused with an H.P. Lovecraft-inspired atmosphere, *AITD* combines puzzle-solving and combat into a smooth, real-time experience. With clues culled from the numerous books and parchments spread liberally throughout the mansion, you set about solving some devilishly tricky—and some decidedly not-so-tricky—puzzles. It's all great fun, with a bad guy located around almost every corner and plenty of chills. The polygonal graphics may turn off some people, but there's just no denying that this is some of the best gameplay ever to hit the PC market.

After the rousing success of *Alone in the Dark*, it was only a matter of time before the sequel, *Alone in the Dark 2*, arrived. Most features of the original game are preserved: the graphics are top-notch, the animation smooth, and the puzzles challenging.

While the original *Alone in the Dark* had you confronting ghosts and ghouls in a haunted mansion, *AITD2* has you battling undead pirates in a garden maze, a mansion, and a pirate ship. The eerie, Lovecraftian feel of the original isn't as prevalent, and the sequel has the more predictable feel of a shoot-em-up rather than a journey into the unknown.

That's not to say that *AITD2* is a mediocre game. In fact, lack of atmosphere aside, *AITD2* is great adventure game. This time, Edward Carnby, the "Private Eye of the Unknown," hears of the kidnapping of Grace Edwards, a young woman being held prisoner in Hell's Kitchen, a mansion overlooking the Pacific. Of course, heroic Edward heads on in, blowing open the front gate with a bomb. After killing the gatehouse guard, Edward finds a Thompson machine gun and a loading-clip, and enters the garden maze.

After solving a few effortless puzzles, Edward finally roots into Hell's Kitchen itself, and the baddies cook up plenty of recipes for pandemonium. A surprising twist on the game is the Santa Claus costume you discover in the basement. Put it on, and you'll gain the trust of a short chef who won't betray Santa to the guards. Seeing ol' Saint Nick gunning down rows of gangsters with a Thompson is just heaps o' fun. Another twist is that you also must play as Grace, rescuing Edward several times during the game.

The polygonal characters, full-screen action, and moody soundtrack are all here from the original game. Added to the CD-ROM version is the spoken dialogue (all of which would probably fill half a page) and the reading of the lengthy books, parchments, and papers you'll find in Hell's Kitchen.

Both *Alone in Dark* games are terrific fun. While the first ranks high in scariness and atmosphere, the second is more action oriented. If they were movies, the first would be akin to *The Haunting*, and the second closer to the *Evil Dead*. Together, they make a great double feature.

Castle of the Winds: A Question of Vengeance

Who's It From? SaadaSoft and Epic MegaGames

Where Is It? X:\WINGAMES\ CASTLE

How Do I Use It? Run CASTLE1.EXE in Windows.

What Do I Get? Volume 1

What Am I Missing? Volume 2 and hint sheet.

How Much? $25.00

How Do I Order? Epic MegaGames, 354 NE Greenwood Ave., Ste. 108, Bend, OR 97701-4631. (800) 972-7434.

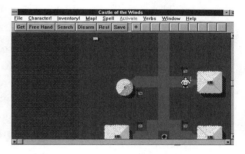

Castle of the Winds is a somewhat crude, but amiably accessible, role-playing adventure for Windows. This alone is noteworthy: few RPGs are designed for Windows. The graphics are flat top-down views of a simplified landscape of hills and dungeons. You assume the role of a young hero out to avenge the murder of his godparents, and at the same time, trying to learn about his true past. The land is filled with monsters, treasure, and traps, and you have to learn spells and develop fighting skills to win. *Castle of the Winds* is no *Ultima*, but it's a diverting little adventure for those who enjoy Windows gaming.

Sam & Max Hit the Road

Who's It From? LucasArts

Where Is It? X:\DOSDEMO\ SAM_MAX\SAMDEMO

How Do I Use It? Type SAMDEMO at DOS prompt, or PLAYDEMO for sound.

What Do I Get? Interactive demo.

How Much? $59.95 CD-ROM

How Do I Order? LucasArts Games, P.O. Box 10307, San Rafael, CA 94912. (800) STAR WARS.

It's fun! It's violent! It's wildly antisocial! Yes, it's *Sam & Max Hit the Road*, the latest CD-ROM laugh-fest from LucasArts. Based on Steve Purcell's comic book, this gem is one of the funniest and most sadistic titles you'll ever play.

Sam and Max, a dog and a rabbit with attitudes, have been hired by a local carnival to help retrieve Bruno the Bigfoot and Trixie the Giraffe-Necked Girl from a British country and western singer/kidnapper. The ensuing quest will take Sam and Max to the seamy underbelly of America—tourist traps such as the World's Largest Ball of Twine, the Celebrity Vegetable Museum, and a converted Mt. Rushmore where you can bungee jump out of your favorite president's proboscis.

All is presented in standard adventure-game style, except LucasArts' usual point-and-click interface has been replaced with a new icon interface which resembles Sierra's. The interface can be kinda clunky at times, but with a little practice you'll be whizzing around the screen like a pro.

Every screen has a gag, which is more than you can say for most sitcoms. Maybe it's the dead animal heads that come to life and recite a moronic limerick about famed naturalist John Muir, as the word "Edutainment" flashes madly on the screen. Or maybe it's just Sam and Max's infatuation with wanton destruction. In any case, *Sam & Max* features great voice acting, from Sam's flatfoot articulation to Max's Bronx drawl, making this a true "interactive cartoon."

Sam and Max's puzzles range from simple to incredibly devious, with the real stumpers saved for the end. Thankfully, the hint book is enclosed with the CD version, including a full walkthrough and object list, along with plenty of Steve Purcell's manic doodles of the crimefighting duo.

Sam & Max Tips

Here are a few pointers to get you started.

- There isn't much to do upstairs, but you might want to check out the mouse holes. Then go out to the street.

- Look for your contact. No, not there. Look lower. (Yes, it's the cat.) "Use" Max with the cat.

- You'll need to get to the carnival. Use the police car parked on the street.

- Lose all your stuff? Check the Lost and Found tent and talk to the Cone of Tragedy operator.

Alright, that's enough hints. Jeeze, go play the game!

As if this wasn't enough, *Sam & Max* also features several "mini-games!" Yes, now you play *Car Bomb* against Max. It's a *Battleship* rip-off, but instead of boats, you have different motor vehicles, trampolines, bombs, and tactical nukes. And don't forget *Highway Surfing*, where Max hops atop the squad car and jumps incoming road signs. Finally, there's *Wak-A-Rat*, where you pound rodents with a giant mallet. Fun!

Day of the Tentacle

Who's It From? LucasArts

Where Is It? X:\DOSDEMO\DOTT

How Do I Use It? Run DOTTDEMO at the DOS prompt.

What Do I Get? Interactive demo.

How Much? $49.95

How Do I Order? LucasArts Games, P.O. Box 10307, San Rafael, CA 94912. (800) STAR WARS.

Just when you thought that LucasArts had topped *Monkey Island 2* with *Indiana Jones and the Fate of Atlantis*, along comes *Day of the Tentacle*, a game that once again proves that LucasArts is the reigning king of the graphic adventure games.

DOTT is actually the sequel to *Maniac Mansion*, which some of us old-timers may well recall. What made *Mansion* unique was that you had control of three kids at the same time throughout a spooky old house—if one was stuck somewhere, the other two could come to his or her rescue.

In the sequel, one of crazy Doctor Fred's Purple Tentacles has gotten loose and takes over the world by making a constitutional amendment that turns humans into slaves. Doctor Fred calls in three teenagers to stop the threat, and sends 'em back in time in Chron-O-Johns (Porta-Potty time machines) to end Purple Tentacle's menace before he can even start. Of course, something in the space/time continuum goes awry, and the three teens are plopped into three different time periods. Bernard, the nerdy hero, remains in the present; Hoagie, a heavy-metal roadie, is transported 200 years in the past; and Laverne, a psychotic med student, is sent 200 years into the future.

Of course, the whole plot is just a set-up for outrageous jokes and a handful of puzzles. And these puzzles aren't of the absurd *use-the-mayonnaise-on-the-totem-pole* variety of *Fate of Atlantis*. Instead, most are pretty easy, and none will leave you stumped for long. A welcome addition is that the characters can "flush" objects to each other with the Chron-O-Johns, making almost all objects available to the kids.

Graphics are obviously inspired by Chuck Jones' early Warner Brothers cartoons. The animation is rubbery and fluid, with sproinging eyeballs, swelling hamsters in microwaves, and exploding cigars. LucasArts' iMuse soundtrack also sounds like the stuff you hear on Saturday morning and is continuous throughout the game.

DOTT is hilarious, laugh-out-loud fun. Since the puzzles aren't as hard as LucasArts' other offerings, it's easily played by anyone, especially those new to the genre. If you have the slightest interest in adventure gaming, this is a true gem.

☆ Indiana Jones and the Fate of Atlantis ☆

Who's It From? LucasArts Entertainment

Where Is It? X:\DOSDEMO\INDY

How Do I Use It? Type PLAYFATE at the DOS prompt.

What Do I Get? Interactive demo.

How Much? $49.95

How Do I Order? LucasArts Games, P.O. Box 10307, San Rafael, CA 94912. (800) STAR WARS.

Before *Sam & Max Hit the Road*, before *Day of the Tentacle* (but after *Monkey Island*—keep it straight), LucasArts made one of their best adventures: *Indiana Jones and the Fate of Atlantis*.

LucasArts had done adventure games before, but all the elements—story, writing, graphics, sound, design, and style—really came together in *Fate*. First of all, you have a recognizable character from the movies and the chance to actually *be* Indy through an all-new adventure. Then, you have the terrific Lucas interface, which reduced all the actions—talk, take, use, and so on—to a few simple icons. The writing is top-notch, with snappy dialog and a ripping good adventure story solidly in the Indiana Jones tradition.

Most unique of all, however, are the three "paths" you can take in playing the game. At a certain point in the game, you can choose either the Team path, in which the lovely psychic Sofia accompanies you on the adventure and helps out with puzzles; the Wits path, in which you go it alone and have to tough out all the puzzles yourself; or the Fists path, which has more action sequences. Whichever path you choose, there will be scenes that are wholly unique to that path, adding substantially to replayability.

And what's the adventure? Well, the Nazis are at it again, plumbing the depths of mythology for a dark secret to help them win the war. That secret lies in the lost city of Atlantis, and Indy must find it before the Nazis do. Along the way there are fiendish Nazis trying to stop him, supernatural powers waiting to be unleashed, tricky puzzles to solve, and a romantic interest to be avoided.

It's all ripping good fun, with tongue firmly in cheek and a rip-roaring pulp fiction feel. And the CD-ROM version is a full-talkie! (No, Harrison Ford didn't do it, they got a sound-alike.) As usual, this is a top-flight LucasArts project.

Gabriel Knight: The Sins of the Fathers

Who's It From? Sierra On-Line

Where Is It? X:\DOSDEMO\ GKNIGHT

How Do I Use It? Type GABRIEL at the DOS prompt.

What Do I Get? Interactive demo.

How Much? $59.95

How Do I Order? Sierra On-Line, P.O. Box 600, Coarsegold, CA 93614.

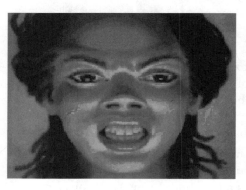

Gabriel Knight is not sure where his life is going. The bookstore his father left him isn't doing so well, and his writing career seems stalled by a severe case of writer's block. For inspiration and material, he starts investigating a series of murders in the French Quarter. His poking around leads him to a voodoo subculture, filled with dangerous characters and strange happenings. Slowly, he begins to learn of his own mysterious heredity, and of his destiny. As a direct descendent of a family of old German *Shattenjäger*, or shadow hunters, he is fated to hunt down and destroy supernatural evil in all its forms.

As with all adventure games, you travel through various locations, questioning characters, picking things up, and uncovering new parts of the story. As you move from place to place over a stylized map, some questions are answered, and new questions arise. Danger seems to lurk everywhere, and there are even some action sequences to spice things up a bit. The story takes you as far afield as Germany and Africa, and introduces more well-rounded characters than are usually seen in adventure games.

The only way to play this is on CD-ROM, where a full cast of professional voice-actors add to the drama. Tim Curry, Efrem Zimbalist Jr., Michael Dorn, and Mark Hamill all lend their talents to fleshing out some already intriguing characters.

Voodoo, witchcraft, the curse of heredity: this is the stuff of which horror is made, and *Gabriel Knight* has them all in abundance. The first of a projected series, *Gabriel Knight: The Sins of the Fathers* takes Sierra's traditional adventure game format into the dark underside of New Orleans for an effective and involving tale of terror.

Freddy Pharkas— Frontier Pharmacist

Who's It From? Sierra On-Line

Where Is It? X:\DOSDEMO\FREDDY

How Do I Use It? Type SIERRA at the DOS prompt.

What Do I Get? Interactive demo.

How Much? $29.95

How Do I Order? Sierra On-Line, P.O. Box 600, Coarsegold, CA 93614.

Freddy Pharkas may just be a computer game version of *Blazing Saddles*, but it's a funny one at that. Created by Al Lowe, the man behind the *Leisure Suit Larry* series, *Freddy* was one of the three funniest games I've played in the past year. (The other two were *Day of the Tentacle* and *Sam and Max Hit the Road*.) Comedy on computer ain't easy. It has to affect a cartoon-like quality,

and not only is that difficult to properly achieve in a game, but it also requires a fair deal of talent, or the results can be dire. Happily, *Freddy* isn't dire.

The year is 1888, and things in Coarsegold, California aren't faring too well. First, the gold gave out. Then, a scheming crook finds out that the land the settlers have built their homes on is worth quite a fair amount of dough. He's determined to grab the land, and it seems like he might have the sheriff's help in the job. After the sheriff closes down all the businesses, people start fleeing, and it looks like the town may just fold up and die. But prairie folk are a hearty lot, and they are determined to stick it out, despite a series of mishaps and plagues designed to make their lives miserable.

Enter Freddy Pharkas. Once the best shot in St. Louis, Freddy lost his nerve—and an ear—one day in a shootout with Kenny the Kid. Thereafter, Freddy dedicated his life to his to passion: pharmacology. Fresh out of pharmacy school, he heads out to Coarsegold to take over their sole pharmacy, only to find the town breathing its last. Undaunted, Freddy sets about restoring the people to health and thwarting the bad guys' evil plans. Plagues of snails, flatulent horses, and a diarrheal populace challenge his skills as a pharmacist, but Freddy and his Indian companion (Srini Lalkaka Bagdnish, from New Delhi) are up to the task.

Dragonsphere

Who's It From? MicroProse

Where Is It? X:\DOSDEMO\DRAGON

How Do I Use It? Type DRAGON at the DOS prompt.

What Do I Get? Interactive demo.

How Much? $59.95

How Do I Order? MicroProse Entertainment Software, 180 Lakefront Dr., Hunt Valley, MD 21030-2245. (410) 771-1151.

MicroProse is relatively new to the world of graphic adventures, and though they've only produced a handful, all have had their merits. Oddly enough, they never seem to get much credit for producing involving, effective adventures with a workable interface, while most kudos go to Sierra On-Line and LucasArts. There's nothing particularly inventive about their MADS interface—it's clearly inspired by LucasArts' engine—but it works so smoothly that you begin to forget you're playing a game. Their graphics are dependable, if not as inspired and zany as those produced by LucasArts, and their story, character interaction, and puzzles are just right. Elements like these made *Rex Nebular and the Cosmic Gender Benders* a genuinely fun—and funny— game, and provided some great moments in the flawed *Phantom of the Opera*. (Note to game makers: *please lose the mazes*, they're a drag.)

All these elements are at work in *Dragonsphere*, which was largely ignored when it was released in a disk version. It's now out on CD-ROM with full voice support, and it's worth a look. The story centers around Callash, the king of the realm, who must find a way to prevent the evil wizard Sanwe from escaping his magical prison and wreaking havoc on the world. You control Callash as he makes his way into the countryside, meeting the other races and creatures that occupy the world and searching for a way to deal with Sanwe. The evocation of these other races, and the interaction with them as Callash tries to forge new alliances, make for an entertaining game. All the standard adventure game functions are here: you talk through dialog trees, collect objects, solve puzzles, and explore the land. Since there are no new interface "tricks" to master, you can concentrate on learning about this rich and detailed world and helping Callash on his mission.

Return to Zork

Who's It From? Activision

Where Is It? X:\ACTIVISN

How Do I Use It? Type INSTALL at the DOS prompt.

What Do I Get? Interactive demo.

How Much? $69.95

How Do I Order? Activision, 11440 San Vincente Blvd., Los Angeles, CA 90049. (800) 477-3650.

There's an easy way to tell how long a person has been computer gaming: just ask them if they remember Infocom games. If you get a slightly nostalgic smile, it means they've been gaming for, well, for as long there have *been* computer games. Infocom games such as *Hitchhiker's Guide to the Galaxy*, *The Leather Goddesses of Phobos*, and, of course, the *Zork* games were based around text parsers. That is, you got a text description of what you were "seeing" and responded by typing things like PICK UP RUBBER HOSE and GO WEST. They allowed you to game within your imagination, seeing the scene with your mind's eye. The most interesting thing about Infocom games for me is that I still have definite *images* in my head from them, as if they were graphical games. I can still *see* scenes from *The Lurking Horror* and *Hitchhiker*, which only ever existed in my mind. That certainly says something for their power.

Obviously, many people felt the same way, for they responded to *Return to Zork*, the first graphical *Zork* game, with such enthusiasm that it became one of the most successful titles of the year. Activision bought up the rights to the Infocom games, including *Zork*, and turned it into a landmark CD-ROM product. Along with *The 7th Guest*, *Myst*, and *Rebel Assault*, it was one of the first games to really show what CD-ROM could do. With good graphic imaging, video, and audio, it was certainly a technical leap, but it was also a solidly playable and entertaining game.

Return to Zork takes place 700 years *after* the last *Zork*, and the world has moved on. The problem? It appears that not all the evil magic has been destroyed, and it's up to you to travel into the underground empire of Zork and save it from the evil forces arrayed against it. Not only does *RTZ* boast a fully interactive world (you can talk to people and pick up and use objects), but it's also fully multimedia: all character roles are performed by professional actors and there is no onscreen text. Activision has brought an old and fondly remembered game world into the modern gaming arena without a hitch, preserving the off-kilter sense of humor and puzzle solving that distinguished the originals. It's one of those titles that makes you glad to own a CD-ROM.

Star Trek: 25th Anniversary and Judgment Rites

Who's It From? Interplay Productions

Where Is It? See the "Trek Demos" box (opposite page).

How Do I Use It? See the "Trek Demos" box.

What Do I Get? Interactive demo.

How Much? $49.95

How Do I Order? Interplay Productions, 17922 Fitch Ave., Irvine, CA 92714. (800) INTERPLAY.

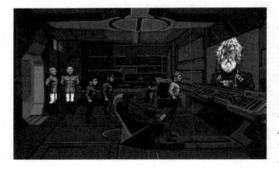

Until recently, the only PC incarnations of *Star Trek* have been some average text and graphic adventures and a shareware strategy title, so when Interplay announced its classic Trek games, Trekkies had cause to rejoice. *Star Trek: 25th Anniversary* and *Judgment Rites* puts you in the captain's chair through a series of adventures firmly in the spirit of the show.

Interplay has done a good job with both games, giving each numerous "Episodes" with their own distinct plots. For most of the game, you'll find yourself controlling the crew with an icon-driven, point-and-click interface that works just fine once you get used to it. During space battle sequences, you get to control the *Enterprise*, which zips around like an X-Wing or Kilrathi fighter, while I seem to recall Mr. Scott's *Enterprise* handling like a pregnant water-buffalo. The adventure-game portions of the *Star Trek* are strong in plot and character interaction, and some of the puzzles are real stumpers, making for a challenging game. Graphics and game "sets" are suitably Sixties in color and design, but, oddly enough, the characters sometimes look like pixelized midgets up close.

All the *Star Trek* characters are here, and if you buy the *25th Anniversary CD-ROM* you'll be treated to the *original* cast performing their lines. Though their performances seem a bit listless at times, hearing William Shatner ("I ... can't ... believe it"), Leonard Nimoy ("Fascinating"), DeForest Kelly ("He's dead, Jim!"), Mr. Scott ("She kent gew annee faster, captin!"), and the rest is enough to make you smile nostalgically.

If you buy *Judgment Rites* on floppies, you'll be amazed by the utter size of it. *Rites* ships on *eleven* disks. This means you better make sure that no thunderstorms are moving into the area, since you'll need "1.5 hours to install," according to the manual. Yikes! And if you think that speech packs are a rip-off, get ready. *Rites* has an optional Movie and Sound Pack that adds several minutes of rendered spaceships (and 10 more megs to your hard drive).

All in all, both *Trek* games will certainly satisfy the Trekkies in the audience, particularly those who recall the brief animated *Trek* series of the 1970s. The prospect of controlling some of television's best known characters should be enough to lure even non-Trekkies to Interplay's fine series.

Star Trek Demos!

We've included both *Star Trek* demos: *25th Anniversary CD-ROM* and *Judgment Rites*.

The STARTREK directory features the largest demo in *Games Extravaganza*, *Star Trek: 25th Anniversary CD-ROM*, which features all the Classic Trek actors performing their parts! If your computer can handle it, you'll find this massive demo in the STARTREK subdirectory. Just run it by typing STARTREK.

The directory RITES is where you can find the *Judgment Rites* demo, which can be run by typing RITES. There is no voice support for this demo.

Mystic Towers

Who's It From? Apogee

Where Is It? X:\DOSHARE\ TOWERS

How Do I Use It? Type TOWERS at the DOS prompt.

What Do I Get? One tower and one apprentice.

What Am I Missing? Twelve towers, new enemies, cheat keys, bonus game, cheats, and manual.

How Much? $24.95

How Do I Order? Apogee, 3960 Broadway, Suite 235, Garland, TX 75043. (800) APOGEE1.

Mystic Towers is another cute shareware game from Apogee aimed at a decidedly younger audience. But instead of being a platform game, it's presented from a *Ultima VIII*-style three-quarters perspective as your character, a frail wizard-type, traverses the towers looking for treasure and bad guys. No new ground has been broken in the graphics department, but *Mystic Towers* does have a fun, cartoonish feel. The sound is nicely executed, and though the interface can be clumsy at times, it becomes manageable after you've been using it for a while. The viewing perspective does present some occasional problems because you can't always tell where you are. This problem is especially magnified when you use keyboard control: I kept getting creamed by monsters because I wasn't *exactly* in the right position. On the whole, however, *Mystic Towers* is a nice change from the *Hocus Pocus* + *Duke Nukem* + *Commander Keen* games we've been seeing for so long.

Myst

☆   ☆

Who's It From? Developed by Cyan, released by Broderbund.

Where Is It? X:\WINGAMES\MYST

How Do I Use It? See special instructions on page 146.

What Do I Get? Interactive demo.

How Much? $59.95

How Do I Order? Broderbund, 500 Redwood Blvd., Novato, CA 94948-6121.

Myst was one of the "big four" of the CD-ROM boom, the other three being, of course, *The 7th Guest*, *Rebel Assault*, and *Return to Zork*. They fed a hungry and exponentially growing CD-ROM market, and fed it well, displaying the dazzling possibilities of CD-ROM in images, sounds, and imagination.

Myst is a land reached through a strange book authored by the mysterious Atrus. Open the book, touch the picture, and you are transported to Myst Island, where other magical books are kept in a library. Each book leads to another strange world, but the books are beginning to disappear, and with them the worlds they lead to. Atrus suspects one of his errant sons is responsible, but he too has vanished after throwing the book of Myst into a dimensional rift.

Somehow you have found the book of Myst and are transported to the island. It is up to you to traverse its many locations and strange inventions to learn who is destroying the books. You step through this world in various, gorgeously-rendered images, almost like a living slide show. Few things can be picked up, but many can be manipulated. The objects throughout the island, from the secret doors and living paintings of the library, to a space ship, a toy boat in a fountain, and numerous dials and switches, all need to be manipulated in the proper way to move further in the game. These puzzles can be quite challenging at times, but in solving them you learn ever more about this mysterious land.

Myst is a gentle and evocative fantasy...an imaginary world which seems almost limitless in terms of places to explore and things to do. It's like having Lewis Carroll's looking glass for a computer monitor: allow yourself to fall inside and you'll find grand new landscapes of the imagination.

THE SECRETS OF *MYST*

Myst is a game of exploration and discovery. There is no race to solve the mysteries of the island, and you can't really make a "fatal" mistake. Be warned, however, that the puzzles on this island are devilishly difficult. They'll seem innocuous enough at first glance, but after throwing a few levers and having nothing happen, you'll start becoming desperate. Rest assured, you are not alone. Hints can be found in any number of official (and unofficial) *Myst* hint books, or from online services. Here are a few ideas to get you started.

- You must throw all the "marker switches" at the various locations. This will activate that location on the map in the library. You only need to throw these switches once.

- 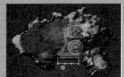 The map in the library is crucial to navigating through and understanding Myst Island. After you throw a marker switch, an icon will appear on this map and light up. You can use this map to rotate the observation tower and see each landmark. Just click on the circular tower icon and hold it: you'll hear it moving, and the line on the map will turn red when it's in position. As the tower rotates, important clues are revealed. Take the elevator up and check each out, writing down the messages or codes for each location.

- The ages you must navigate are the Mechanical, Stoneship, Selenitic, and Channelwood ages. You do this by solving the puzzles throughout Myst and finding the corresponding book. These books are on the shelf in the library, and you can read them for important clues.

- There are two books in the library which, when opened, show a window full of static. There are loose pages beside the books. Pick them up by clicking on them, place them in the books, and you'll get snippets of messages from Atrus's sons, Sirrus and Achenar. They've been locked within the books, and as you find more loose pages, more of the message will come through.

- To reveal the hidden alcove in the gears, set the tower to overlook that location (to the southeast), then find the numbers on the plaque in the tower. They should read *2:40 221*. Set the clock at the other end of the island to 2:40 by rotating the wheels. The small wheel moves the little hand, and the large moves the big hand. When the clock says 2:40, push the red button. A walkway will materialize, allowing you to cross to the island, throw the marker switch, and enter the clock tower.

- Once inside the clock towers, play with the levers until the number reads 2 2  1, top to bottom. Experiment with pulling a lever and letting go, and pulling and holding it. It's not too hard once you find the pattern. When you get the right combinations, you'll hear a grinding sound as gears move to reveal the alcove beneath them. Go there and touch the picture in the book to travel to the Mechanical Age.

- To return to the Library from the Mechanical Age, enter these symbols and hit the red button. A secret panel will slide back to reveal steps leading down. Go down and touch the swirling image in the book.

Myst **Special Instructions**

Given the current makeup of this CD-ROM, the following steps will be required for the *Myst* demo to work. This installation will take about 45 megs on your hard drive. We regret any inconvenience this may cause.

1. Make a new directory on your hard drive called X:\MYSTDEMO by typing MD MYSTDEMO at the DOS prompt or using the Create Directory Command in Windows File Manager.

2. Copy all the files and subdirectories in X:\WINGAMES\MYST on the *Extravaganza* CD-ROM to this new MYSTDEMO directory.

3. Run INSTALL in Windows from the MYSTDEMO directory.

4. Enter X:\MYSTDEMO as the installation directory during install.

5. After installation, open the MYSTDEMO\MYST.INI file with a text editor (such as Notepad) and delete the first line "MystMPCDrive". Then change the line "DRIVE = [drive letter]" to the letter of your hard drive (ie: "DRIVE = C") and save the file.

6. Run the game from the Myst icon in the Program Manager.

FOUR

STRATEGY & WAR GAMES

Strategy gamers are a special breed. They prefer games that are ostensibly quieter, more thoughtful, and more time consuming. Many wargamers are students of history who view games as a natural progression of their interests. And, by extension, we can assume that many *SimCity* players are frustrated urban planners, many *Civilization* players are closet tyrants, and so on. You would think this sort of gamer is more high-minded, more cerebral, somehow *different* than an arcade gamer.

You'd be wrong.

As a hard-core strategy player, I can tell you that, as a group, we're the most bloodthirsty gamers around. We thrive on crushing opponents and stomping their remains into a fine powder, salting their lands, and selling their people into slavery. We won't be satisfied until the entire world is bent under our yoke.

These games have a way of making you that way. Take *Civilization*, for instance. When you begin your first game, you may well be a normal human being looking for a couple hours of diversion. Twenty hours later you're a red-eyed, foaming wreck who won't be happy until you nuke Nepal. The game has had its way with you, and you can't escape it. It has exposed some dark, hitherto unknown aspect of your character.

But there are as many different strategy games as there are different kinds of people. *Civilization* can be played with an enlightened, high-culture edge, or as a ruthless military exercise. You can build a happy, intelligent populace devoted to art and culture, or a war machine to crush the most people in the fastest time possible. Not all games have that diversity, but each is subtly different, and most fall into one of the follow categories.

Historical wargames attempt to model real battles using pieces which stand in for real units. They can exist on a number of levels, from small platoon-level games such as *World War II Battles*, to more complex, historically accurate games such as the *V for Victory* series. A sub-category of this would be *conflict simulators* such as *Harpoon 2*. These aren't modelled on historical scenarios, but use real, contemporary units to play through hypothetical future scenarios.

Global conquest games come in many shades, but all are based around a single unifying principle: *be lord of the world*. These strategy games are often quite complex, as any global conquest must be, and often figure in such elements as managing technical and cultural growth; keeping the people happy; providing food, stability, and entertainment; all while balancing the needs of the military. *Civilization, Master of Orion, Master of Magic,* and numerous others take on this high level of complexity, while titles such as *Global Conquest* or *Risk* focus more on the military element.

Abstract wargames usually have generic units and concepts, but can also use realistically styled units in a more generalized way. For instance, *Empire* uses generic units such as armor, ships, infantry, and so on, without attaching particular values or historical categories to them. Some games fight out "historical" battles in ahistorical fashion, with units only approximating the values of the actual units. *Clash of Steel* from SSI is this type of game.

Economic simulations such as *Detroit, Railroad Tycoon, Theme Park,* and MicroProse's new *Transport Tycoon* and *Pizza Tycoon* are unique and aimed at a select group of people. Not everyone cares to tinker with the insides of a large corporation, or find as much of a thrill in driving competitors into bankruptcy as they do in crushing their armies, but those who do can't get enough. Who doesn't want to try his or her hand at being a tycoon, and make all the decisions that will lead a company to success?

Science-fiction and fantasy wargames share many elements with abstract wargames, yet use the elements of, obviously, science-fiction. Warfare occurs in space rather than on the ground, or uses orcs, trolls, and similar units rather than tanks and infantry. These games might draw unique elements into their strategy, such as spell-casting or raising the dead.

Civilization

☆ ☆

Who's It From? MicroProse	**How Much?** $51.95 (DOS), $57.95 (Windows).
Where Is It? X:\DOSDEMO\CIVRR	
How Do I Use It? Type CIVDEMO at the DOS prompt.	**How Do I Order?** MicroProse Entertainment Software, 180 Lakefront Dr., Hunt Valley, MD 21030-2245. (410) 771-1151.
What Do I Get? Non-interactive demo.	

You remember what it was like the first time. You couldn't get enough. It left you beaten and collapsed in a pool of sweat by the time it was over, near dawn. You knew it could never again be that good, and you knew you had to do it all over again as soon as you could. You didn't think you could ever get enough.

Civilization is capable of affecting people that way. (Well, what did you think I was talking about?) It sinks its Machiavellian claws into you and won't let go until the entire world lays prostrate at your feet. Possibly the single finest computer game ever, *Civilization*'s stature and playability has not diminished one bit in the three years since its initial release. As new users discover computer games, they inevitably find *Civilization* and fall prey to its addictive lure. If you don't already own it, you should.

The premise of this game, designed by MicroProse whiz Sid Meier, is as simple as the box-blurb makes it out to be: build an empire to stand the test of time. You start on a black sea of unexplored territory with a single wagonload of settlers. With these, you will build a city, name it, and set your people to the task of farming, mining, researching, and building new units to use for exploration and conquest. At first you can only build a few different units: militia, settlers, maybe another type of military unit if you start the game with an advanced technology. Resources go toward keeping the populace happy, researching new technologies, and building new units. These units explore new places, found new settlements, and find other civilizations. You can make peace or fight with them, depending upon which course you choose to follow.

CIVILIZATION **STRATEGIES**

Everyone has their own way of winning at *Civilization*, and everyone is sure that their way is the *only* way. Well, so am I. I've offered only a handful here, but volumes can—and have!—been filled with tips on how to play this game. You'll certainly develop your own techniques, but here are a few to start with.

- *Opening Moves:* You begin with one settler and a sea of black. Almost without question, I put down roots as soon as the game starts. I don't move the settler around: I just build my first city and hope for the best. If the land looks completely arid and untenable, then obviously this is not a good idea. But, if you're not generating a planet that is largely dry and rocky, this shouldn't be a problem. The point is to get started building as soon as possible.

- *Scout:* Naturally you start by building a Militia unit. Convential wisdom says this unit should stay put and defend the town. If you build the unit and send it out, the town is basically unprotected and easy pickins. But, since it's still early in the game, you can take some risks. If your town is overrun, you can just start again. So, send your Militia off to scout for your next town location and begin building settlers. Use this Militia unit to scope out an ever-widening circle around your city. If danger lurks nearby in the form of barbarians, have the unit return to town and fortify. It is unlikely that other civilizations will be attacking at this stage.

- *Plan Strategy:* Early on you want to scout because you need to get a feel for how  large a continent you're on, whether it's rich in resources, and whether you'll have to contend with other civilizations vying for the same continent. The results of this scouting will determine much of your early strategy. For example, if you're on a tiny island, you need to start working toward inventing Triremes first, in order to expand to another land mass. If the continent is abandoned except for you, then you can relax your defenses for the initial stage of the game and concentrate on building new cities and developing technology. If another civ is on the continent, then you have to be more careful about defense.

- *Develop the Land:* Put down new cities ASAP, and have these build still more Settlers. Always keep one, and preferably two, Settlers building roads, irrigating, and mining. The roads will be a blessing when quick troop movements become necessary. The irrigation will allow you to use land productively. Try to place new cities where they can exploit both agricultural and mineral resources. Nothing is nicer than a large gold mine or oil well that you can pump for dough when you need it.

- *Keep Your Frontier Defended:* A defense based only on protecting cities is a weak defense. Keep your "front lines" well forward, and stop the enemy *before* they can attack cities.

- *Research Efficiently:* Early on you're going to have to deal with technology and research. The best units to work for early on are Chariots, Catapults and Musketeers. To get Catapults, research Masonry, the Alphabet, and Mathematics. Chariots come with the discovery of the Wheel. Musketeers become available via Masonry, Constructions, Bronze Working, Currency, the Wheel, Engineering, the Alphabet, Writing, Code of Laws, Literacy, Invention, Iron Working, and Gunpowder. These are the paths of discovery that will lead to a potent military force.

- *Try New Governments:* Too many players take the easy way out and stick with Despotism because it's the easiest way to wage war. This is futile, and will ultimately result in a muscle-bound but economically stagnant state. Growth and happiness are the keys to success, and while advanced governments come with their problems (it often becomes much harder to keep people happy and wage war, and units cost more to maintain), they will yield better results. Monarchies, for example, yield higher production but require more production points to maintain units. Military units away from home in a Democracy make people unhappy, but there is *no* corruption, and both trade and production are at their highest and cities grow more rapidly. Often it's a good idea to switch to another government to feed your coffers and "grow" your cities, then return to an easier form of government.

- *Waging War in a Free Society*: Since the people in free societies like a Republic or Democracy don't like war, they won't let you attack willy-nilly and will accept most treaties even if you reject them. An easy way around this is to be attacked first. Just stick a military unit deep in enemy territory and it will often be attacked, breaking any treaties and allowing you to wage war.

- *Trade and Diplomacy*: Both are too often ignored and both are crucial. Build Caravans to establish complex trade patterns with foreign countries. The increased revenue will support additional maintenance costs as your civilization grows. Build lots of Diplomats and send them into the countryside in order to establish diplomatic ties (important for information on your enemy's size and strength), spy, and sabotage. Proper use of these units can be a deciding factor in victory.

Meanwhile, your technological level is increasing as your scientists work hard to develop new inventions. These technological advances in turn give you more advanced units, and from phalanx and catapults, you work your way up to nuclear missiles and SDI. All the time, you're striving to balance military expansion with keeping your populace happy. You build structures in your cities to entertain them (coliseums), make them more content (churches), and improve the standard of living (aqueducts). There are also numerous Great Wonders to build, such as the Hanging Gardens or a Great Pyramid, and these also exert a peaceable influence on your people, as well as adding to the value of your culture. Build roads and rail lines, irrigate the plains, and mine the hills: the world is yours to shape and conquer. Heck, you can even now conquer in Windows, with the newly enhanced and improved *Civilization for Windows*.

Some games you can play and replay indefinitely, and *Civilization* is one of the few computer games like this. It is so revolutionary in design that its long shadow continues to fall upon any strategy games which come after it, and it will likely be played as long as computer games are played.

Civilization Editor

Who's It From? Carlos Medeiros

Where Is It? X:\WINGAMES\CIVEDIT

How Do I Use It? Run SETUP from Windows.

How Much? Free

How Do I Order? Send comments to Carlos Medeiros, P.O. Box 4219, Fall River, MA 02722.

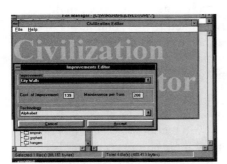

This is a simple and effective windows editor for *Civilization* (DOS version). You can change many of elements of game play, such as unit cost, unit value, unit strength, technological improvements, and other aspects. With a quite easy-to-use interface and powerful range of functions, Carlos Medeiros' *Civilization Editor* lets you tweak play any way you want.

☆ Railroad Tycoon Deluxe ☆

Who's It From? MicroProse

Where Is It? X:\DOSDEMO\CIVRR

How Do I Use It? Type TYCOON at the DOS prompt.

What Do I Get? Non-interactive demo.

How Much? $25.95

How Do I Order? MicroProse Entertainment Software, 180 Lakefront Dr., Hunt Valley, MD 21030-2245. (410) 771-1151.

This is another older title that I simply could not leave out. The original *Railroad Tycoon*, designed by Sid Meier, was released so long ago I can't even recall the year. Reagan might have still been president, however. Last year, MicroProse gave *Railroad Tycoon* a much needed facelift and retitled it *Railroad Tycoon Deluxe*, with new graphics, new trains, and new regions with unique needs, thus generating fresh interest in a title that revolutionized computer game design.

When it came out, it galvanized the gaming community with its open-ended, engrossingly detailed approach to strategic gaming. What's more, *Railroad Tycoon*

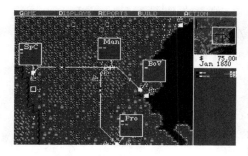

was not a wargame, but an *economic* simulation. As a budding entrepreneur in the nineteenth century, you have the entire fruit of the industrial revolution for the taking, if you're clever enough. The world economy is being driven by the growth of railroads, which is the only way products can be moved from supplier to factory, and from factory to consumer. Ore, food, mail, people: everything moves by rail. New territories are opened by rail, and new towns spring up along the tracks to trade and to service the railroads. The cutthroat robber barons are staking their claims across the country, and you have to lay out the most profitable rail lines, build trains and stations, and start hauling.

You begin as an investor with a bit of capital in the bank and the ability to make simple railroad networks. By hauling goods from place to place, you make money to expand your financial empire. As new train technologies are developed, you can move more goods at a faster speed, thereby increasing revenues. In *Railroad Tycoon Deluxe*, you can build in North or South America, Eastern or Western United States, Europe and Africa, and each has its own requirements for growth. (In Africa, for instance, you need to control the port cities.) As the years roll by, you are kept apprised of your (and your competitors') changing fortunes, as well as the history of the times.

We may be in the middle of a multimedia frenzy, where technology is king and games that aren't flashy and splashy often get ignored, but the simple fact is that nothing can top superior gameplay. *Railroad Tycoon* may have been eclipsed technologically by games with better graphics, but few new titles can equal its depth of play or sheer fun factor. There's a lot of meat to this game and to its progeny, *Civilization*. (*Railroad Tycoon*'s design was the jumping off point for Meier's *Civilization* design.) Classics never die, and *Railroad Tycoon* is proof.

Detroit

Who's It From? Impressions Software

Where Is It? X:\DOSDEMO\DETROIT

How Do I Use It? Type DETROIT at the DOS prompt.

What Do I Get? Interactive demo of

commercial release.

How Much? $69.95

How Do I Order? Impressions Software, 7 Melrose Dr., Farmington, CT 06032.

Impressions does well what few companies ever do at all: economic simulations. Oh, you can certainly look to MicroProse's *Railroad Tycoon* as an example of an economic simulation, but can you name another?

"An economic simulation?" I hear you saying. "What a drag!"

Ah, but you'd be wrong. With *Air Bucks*, Impressions put the construction of an entire airline in your hands. *You* became the CEO of a fledgling company, and you had to make the decisions that would make your company grow in a realm of cutthroat competition. It wasn't a wholly successful game, but Impressions took what they learned and ran with it.

The result is *Detroit*, an honest-to-god simulation of that most American of institutions, the auto industry. You start the game with some capital (how much determines how hard the game will be), and a series of offices for running and managing the company. Begin by designing a car, controlling the specifications,

---

DETROIT HINTS

In the beginning, try hiring as many technicians and assembly workers as possible. Pay technicians around $70 and assembly workers about $90 (assembly workers have better unions). Begin with newspaper and billboard advertisements, to the tune of between $100 and $175 each. Family sedans sell in the beginning, but sporty little hot rods will soon sell like hotcakes. Pickup trucks are dodgy, as are vans. Expand to new North American markets quickly.

The Archive is where you store all your car designs.

Plan your marketing strategy and buy advertising.

Generate graphs and progress reports, handle personnel, and contact the bank.

Design new car models.

Assign researchers to R&D to develop new technologies.

Open new factories and sales offices, set prices, and assign workers.

color, shape, and all the features to be included. At first, you'll have a hand-brake and engine, and that's about it.

As you hire scientists, and allot money for research, you can develop improvements such as new engines, body types, safety features, and other doo-dads to separate your car from the pack. Give it a name, take it for a spin on the test track, hire some workers, and start building it! Pretty soon, you'll be advertising, opening new dealerships, and watching your income go either up or down. (Up is preferable.)

This is a challenging game, especially for those who like to tinker and spend money on things like "stadium advertising." So many factors go into making a successful company, and so much is riding on making the proper decisions, that the game can easily be played over and over again from different angles.

Hmmm, what other industries are there for Impressions to take on? How about the entertainment business? Or the space program? Or international shipping? Or even health care?

Theme Park

Who's It From? Bullfrog/Electronic Arts

Where Is It? X:\DOSDEMO\PARK

How Do I Use It? Type PARK at the DOS prompt

What Do I Get? Interactive demo

How Much? $49.95

How Do I Order? Electronic Arts, 1450 Fashion Island Blvd., San Mateo, CA 94403.

This is one of the goofiest games I've ever seen, and I mean that as a compliment.

Think of it: you're a budding entrepreneur with a little bit of capital and a desire to enter the cutthroat theme park business. Competitors lurk in the shadows, waiting to buy up shares in your growing theme park and take over. Ill-maintained rides sometimes explode, throwing children in all directions. New rides must be developed and new concessions built and stocked. Thunderstorms threaten to drive people away, as do poor restroom facilities, boring rides, and long lines.

Sound like a recipe for disaster? In other hands it may well have been, but as created by the inimitable British developers Bullfrog, creators of *Populous* and *Syndicate*, it's a lot of fun.

Beginning the game with a bit of cash and a map of the world, you choose a place to build your first theme park. (England is the only place low-rent enough. Figures.) With a street rolling by out front and a gate keeping out the thronging masses, you're given some time to place a couple of rides and concessions on a level field, build some paths and bathrooms, hire some workers, and then let the little "peeps" (kids) into the park. The first few rides are a mixed bag: a plain bouncy castle, a haunted house, a teacup merry-go-round. But it's enough for the kids at first, and as you pump more money into developing more rides, your park expands. You have to make sure the peeps can get to the rides via well-organized paths, and make sure they can get out again without getting lost. Since rides are always breaking down and people are always making a mess, workmen need to be on hand to fix things and park workers to clean up.

158   Tom McDonald's PC Games Extravaganza

THE RIDES OF *THEME PARK*

If you put enough into research in *Theme Park,* more and more rides will become available for building. In the CD-ROM version, you can even ride a number of them in some dizzying animated scenes. Here are just a few you'll find if you play long enough!

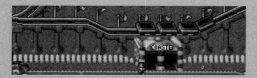

Build your roller-coaster...

...and ride it!

Shuttle Ride

The Parasols

Plane Flyer

The Big Wheel

Ride the Tubes!

In the Haunted House

There are lots of financial tricks to play with the concessions. You can make the food too salty so the peeps buy more soda, and add more ice to the soda so it lasts longer. Of course, if the peeps catch on, they'll be mighty unhappy. How do you know? Well, peeps walk around with a little thought balloon over their heads, expressing thoughts such as "I'm hungry, there's not enough to eat," and "You're making too much profit." If the bathrooms aren't kept clean enough or are too close to the rides, the little beggars start puking all over the sidewalk. Labor disputes, weather changes, and hostile competitors make sure you're constantly on your toes.

A number of users had a few small problems with some elements of *Theme Park*. Employees seem a little dense and need to be micromanaged a bit too much for a game of this type. This can make things mighty tough, and frankly it gets pretty hard to keep up with the park on the more difficult levels. Control is also a little finicky, and you may find yourself accidentally laying sidewalk in pretzel shapes all over the place. But these are quibbles. *Theme Park* has some truly fun and imaginative elements, and the new CD-ROM version fixes some bugs and even allows you to try out your own rides!

☆ SimCity 2000 ☆

Who's it From? Maxis

Where is It? X:\DOSDEMO\SC2000

How Do I Use It? Type SC2000 at the DOS prompt.

What Do I Get? Interactive demo.

How Much? $69.95

How Do I Order? Maxis, 2 Theatre Square, Orinda, CA 94563-3346.

There are bad games, there are good games, and there are compulsions. *SimCity* was a compulsion. *SimCity 2000* is a downright addiction. If you don't believe me, ask anyone who's stayed up all night zoning, rezoning, building roads, raising taxes, and altogether trying to make the miserable existence of his or her wretched, ungrateful little Sims just a trifle more pleasant.

Why we bother, I'll never know. You build them a park, but they want a zoo; you build them a zoo, and they scream for a stadium. You build them trains, and they *still* clog up the highways by driving

IT'S GOOD TO BE THE MAYOR

Being a SimMayor has its perks, that's for sure. Not the least of them are the rewards given out as your population grows. When your population reaches certain sizes, you can build each of the following structures. Many people choose to set them in a prominent place in the city, surrounded by a bit of open space, or maybe some trees.

Here's what you can expect if you're good at making your city thrive. (The *Population* figure is the level at which these structures become available.)

Population: 2,000
Reward: The people build you a nice Mayor's House.

Population: 10,000
Reward: You get to build a City Hall.

Population: 30,000
Reward: SimWorld makes your city the state capitol and you get a statue!

Population: 60,000
Reward: Offer of a Military Base (Air Force, Army, Navy or Missile Silos). Bases boost the economy and the army is available for disasters, but there is also an increase in crime near the base.

Population: 90,000
Reward: The Llama Dome! This is an all-purpose entertainment and civic center, used for weddings and bungee-jumping.

Population: 120,000
Reward: You can build "arcologies:" large, self-contained "cities-in-a-building" where thousands of people can live in a limited space. The first kind is only available after the year 2000, and a new type becomes available each 50 years.
Plymouth Arco: Holds 55,000 people.
Forest Arco: Holds 30,000 people (shown at the left).
Darco (De-urbanized Arcological Construct): Holds 45,000 people.
Launch Arco: Holds 65,000 people, and, no, it doesn't launch.

SimCities!

For owners of *SimCity 2000*, we've included ten or so SimCities for you to check out. Make 'em grow or just destroy them. Each is interesting in its own way. You'll find them in the X:\DOSDEMO\SC2000\CITIES directory.

---

to work. Cut down a few trees to make room for some nice new developments, and they whine that you're destroying the natural habitat of the bull moose. Then, once in rare while, they'll actually give you a statue or a new place to live. But don't hold your breath.

Thus goes the life of a SimMayor.

You begin *SimCity 2000* much like you did the original: with an expanse of land—randomly generated or custom sculpted using a terrain editor—and enough money to start zoning your town, wiring it for electricity, and building roads. You lay down small grids of either densely or lightly developed industrial, commercial, and residential zones. Once these areas are electrified and connected with roads, the Sims begin moving in. They build houses, start businesses, and raise factories. Soon they need fire and police protection, things to entertain them and, if all is going well, more and more space. If the location and layout are good and the taxes reasonable, your city grows, expands, becomes more upscale, and begins to spread across the maps. Airports, military bases, schools, futuristic "arcologies" (for housing many thousands of people), and all manner of structures can be built, while a variety of others spring up on their own. One business in your commercial zone may be a movie theater playing SimAnt, another might be a diner, and so on. You have to keep people happy, crime down, income high, pollution low, and traffic lights on to get good ratings.

Trust me, it ain't easy, and it costs a fortune in SimTax money, but once you start, you simply *can't* stop until the entire map with covered with the most expensive property imaginable. It's as if accomplishing anything less speaks ill of your character.

SimCity 2000 introduces many new features and enhancements, not the least of which are the fabulous, detailed graphics, expanded access to data about your city, a powerful land editor (you have to buy one separately to edit land in the original), new sound effects, all manner of rewards for the effective SimMayor, and numerous other worthwhile things. This is truly a new version worth getting even if you own the previous version (*especially* if you own the previous version!). It's intelligent, challenging, funny, and imaginative: all qualities to be cherished in computer games. It is rightfully considered one of the finest games—of any type—ever. Way to go, Maxis!

THE *SIMCITY 2000* TOOLBAR

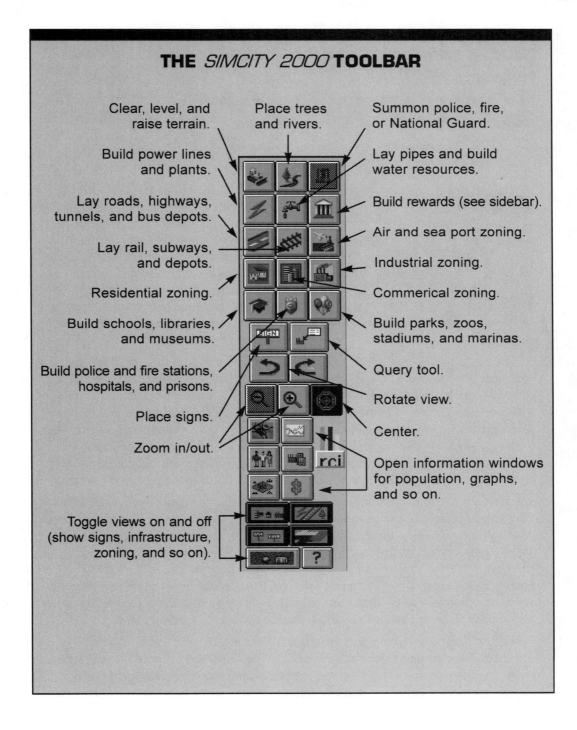

Clear, level, and raise terrain.

Place trees and rivers.

Summon police, fire, or National Guard.

Build power lines and plants.

Lay pipes and build water resources.

Lay roads, highways, tunnels, and bus depots.

Build rewards (see sidebar).

Lay rail, subways, and depots.

Air and sea port zoning.

Industrial zoning.

Residential zoning.

Commerical zoning.

Build schools, libraries, and museums.

Build parks, zoos, stadiums, and marinas.

Build police and fire stations, hospitals, and prisons.

Query tool.

Place signs.

Rotate view.

Zoom in/out.

Center.

Open information windows for population, graphs, and so on.

Toggle views on and off (show signs, infrastructure, zoning, and so on).

Castles II: Siege & Conquest

Who's it From? Interplay

Where is It? X:\DOSDEMO\C2

How Do I Use It? Type C2DEMO at the DOS prompt.

What Do I Get? Interactive demo.

How Much? $59.95

How Do I Order? Interplay Productions, 17922 Fitch Ave., Irvine, CA 92714. (800) INTERPLAY.

In medieval society, castles provided not only protection from enemies, but also became a focal point of culture and society. *Castles II: Siege & Conquest Multimedia*, from Interplay, is a strategy game that captures the nature of this society, where alliances are made and broken, the pope is the supreme holy ruler, borders are constantly shifting, and a few ambitious nobles vie for ultimate power.

You assume the role of a lord with only a small piece of land to your name, and your goal is to become king. By manipulating three tasks—administrative, military, and political—you control all the elements of your growing realm. Each task comes with a certain number of points which you can assign to different needs, and these points grow along with your kingdom. Administrative tasks include rounding up the supplies—gold, iron, wood, and food—necessary to keep things rolling. Raising troops, attacking, and sabotage are some of the military tasks you can perform, while diplomacy, scouting, spying, and trade are handled with the political task allotment.

Eventually, as your kingdom expands, you'll come in contact with your neighbors. You have to conquer new territories to gain the raw materials you need and to protect your borders. To secure these new territories, you build castles. Putting together walls, moats, towers, and other elements are key to effective castle-building, and a good castle will not only afford protection, but also make your people happier. There's enough of a strategy element to keep *Castles II* challenging and interesting, but it's not too difficult for those new to strategy games. Plus, there's an element of palace intrigue, as you make the various decisions facing a medieval lord.

Castles II Multimedia enhances the original *Castles II* by adding a substantial amount of documentary video from the BBC. Video is played full-screen and is simply some of the clearest video I've ever seen on a computer. This video provides not only an excellent introduction to the history of castles and the times in which they were built, but also supplements an extensive online castle reference. Featuring almost a dozen of the most prominent castles throughout the world, this reference includes photos, video, narration, design specs, and weighs the benefits and drawbacks of each. You can drop to this reference from within the castle-building section of the game, choose a historical castle, and order it built. More than that, the gameplay is liberally sprinkled with footage from *Alexander Nevsky* and *The Private Life of Henry VIII* at critical points in the action. A nicely enhanced medieval soundtrack and effective voice acting round out the package, making it a truly exceptional multimedia game.

Interplay could have spiffed up the graphics a bit more, but on the whole this is a great port to CD-ROM, and one of the few that fans of the original should also pick up.

☆ Empire Deluxe ☆

Who's it From? New World Computing

Where is It? X:\DOSDEMO\EMPIRE

How Do I Use It? Type EMDEMO at the DOS prompt.

What Do I Get? Interactive demo.

How Much? $59.95

How Do I Order? New World Computing, P.O. Box 4302, Hollywood, CA 90078-4302.

I've tried to be very careful about which games I mark with an "all-time classic" symbol throughout this book. Too often things are labeled "classics" when they are merely good, and that cheapens the term. Classics are either so new and different that they reshape the field, or they are of such high and unassailable quality that no one can question the designation. The original *Empire* was both of these. It was not only a new and different computer

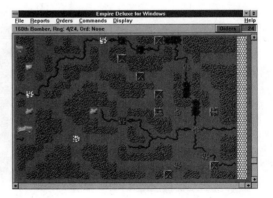

strategy game, it was a new strategy game, period. It pushed the category into a new realm, and you can see its influence quite clearly on games such as *Civilization*. Since classics are reinvented for each generation, as they should be, it was no surprise when designer Mark Baldwin and publisher New World

THE *EMPIRE DELUXE* TOOLBAR

Brushes: Use these to "paint" terrain tiles on the map. The small brush lays one tile, while the large brush lays a 3 X 3 square.

Clear: Clear terrain has no effect on movement.

Water: Only sea or air units may enter water.

River: Armor units lose one movement point. Land units have their defense rating doubled against attack by Armor.

Forest: Armor units lose one movement point. Land units have their defense rating doubled against attack from non-infantry units.

Mountain: Armor may not enter. Land units have their defense rating doubled against attack from non-infantry units.

Rough: Armor units lose one movement point.

Neutral City: Neutral cities have a defense rating of 2. Only friendly cities may be entered.

Player City: Add the attack/defense of any occupying units to the strength of the city.

Infantry: 1/2/2/6

Armor: 2/2/2/12

Fighter: 6(18)/2/2/12

Bomber: 4(24)/2/2/12

Submarine: 2/2/1/24

Destroyer: 3/2/2/24

Cruiser: 2/2/2/42

Battleship: 2/2/2/60

Aircraft Carrier: 2/1/3/48

Transport: 2/1/1/30

Note: The values above are for the Advanced Game. The stats for the units are, in order: *movement points*, *defense*, *attack*, and *time to produce*.

returned to fix up *Empire* and bring it to a whole new generation. And that's exactly what *Empire Deluxe* does.

The concept of *Empire* is quite simple. Up to six opponents compete on varying landscapes with abstracted air, sea, infantry, and armor units. The landscape can be one of many set scenarios, either fanciful or historical, which can be randomly generated each time you play, or can be created by the user with the most powerful wargame editor around. Mountains, plains, forests, rivers, oceans, and cities are the playing field. You might find yourself on a complete, fully mapped landscape, or on a sea of black which you must explore to find the enemy. The size of the battlefield and types of combatants are up to you. If you want to fight an all-sea or all-land battle, you can. Cities produce military units, and are the main targets for attack: capture all the enemies' cities, and you've won.

It's all so pleasantly simple to understand, and so devilishly complex to beat. Things are only made trickier by full modem support, which allows you to fight as many live opponents as your computer can handle. In this kind of play, you can even forge alliances with some players to attack others.

Empire Deluxe is one of the few games that, except for graphics, won't age: between modem play and infinitely varied scenarios, you will *never* run out of fresh strategic challenges. It's available in either a Windows or DOS version, or best of all, since you obviously own a CD-ROM, in the *Empire Deluxe Masters Edition*, which includes *all* versions of *Empire* and *Empire Deluxe* plus add-on scenarios on one CD. If you're reading this section and haven't ever played *Empire*, you're missing one of the true joys of strategy gaming.

Empire Scenarios!

I've put a handful of Empire Deluxe scenarios in the X:\DOSDEMO\EMPIRE\SCE-NARIO directory. Most are by other designers and have been downloaded from CompuServe, and a couple are by me. They include Stalingrad, the Korean War, the Bay of Pigs, a weird attempt at a Corregidor scenario, Israel, and a full-board, five-player slaughterfest. My thanks to the other authors for their fine work!

ABM Command

Who's It From? Kurt Rollins

Where Is It? X:\WINGAMES\ABM

How Do I Use It? Run ABM.EXE in Windows.

What Do I Get? The whole thang.

What Am I Missing? Nada.

How Much? Freeware.

How Do I Order? Send comments to CIS 72040,1607

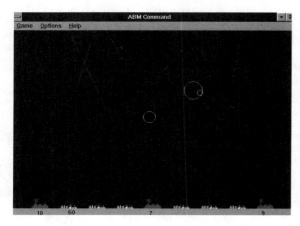

There are so many variants of "Missile Command"-style games that it was difficult to choose the best one. I liked Kurt Rollins' version because it works in Windows and is simple and elegant. This type of game has been popping up on mainframes and has been hacked for years. The point of *ABM Command* and similar games is to intercept all of the nuclear missiles before they hit your town. You can send up counter-missile fire to take out the nukes as they rain down, following their arcs of flight. The game gets faster and the missiles more numerous as you do better, and they get closer and closer to your towns. Try to set your counter-missile fire off in a position to take out more than one nuke. The concussion of your explosion travels outward for some distance, and you can often kill numerous nukes with one well-placed hit.

Destroyer for Windows

Who's It From? Timberline Software

Where Is It? X:\WINGAMES\ DESTROY

How Do I Use It? Run DES4WIN.EXE in Windows.

What Do I Get? The basic game.

What Am I Missing? New versions, sounds, screens, and modem support.

How Much? $20

How Do I Order? Timberline Software, 12558 W. Aqueduct Dr., Littleton, CO 80127-6225. CIS: 71162,2761.

The game of *Battleship*—made into a best-selling board game by Milton Bradley—is a classic pen and paper game that requires only two players and a numbered grid. Each player places a series of differently sized ships (carrier, submarine, battleship, destroyer) in different positions on the grid. They can go in any direction, but they usually take up two to four spaces each. The game is played simply by calling out coordinates on the grid where you think your enemy might have placed his or her ships. If one of your coordinates is a "hit," then you've found a ship, and you keep on firing in that area until that ship sinks.

Like "Missile Command"-style games, "Battleship"-style games are a popular subject for shareware. They're good coffee break specials and don't require complex logorhythms for their artificial intelligence. Of all of them, I found Timberline's variant *Destroyer for Windows* to be the best. Its graphics are quite good, and allow a choice of Pacific or Atlantic oceans, with corresponding Japanese or German symbology for the background screens. When you score a hit on a ship, the corresponding ship in the background image takes a hit and begins to burn. When it's completely destroyed, there's even a little sinking animation. If you're a big Windows user, you'll find yourself playing this one in off-hours without even really thinking about it, so go ahead and register it.

Empire II for Windows

Who's It From? Casey Butler, Viable Software Alternatives

Where Is It? X:\WINGAMES\EMPWIN

How Do I Use It? Run EMPIRE in Windows

How Much? $30

How Do I Order? Viable Software Alternatives, Route 10, Box 360, Carbondale, IL 62901.

Can't get enough of that world conquest! Like *Risk* and *Stratego*, *Empire II* is a simplified game of conquest. Each player is given a country in one of several major regions—North America, South America, Asia, or Europe—and provided with about 50 military units. This country may then attack any of its neighbors by selecting them with the menu button. The attack begins and troops fight until one or the other is completely destroyed, or until a retreat. If you win, you can then occupy the defeated nation and continue attacking other countries until your troops are spread too thin to make any further attacks possible. After you've made all your moves and hit the "pass" button, the opponents make theirs, and you're equipped with more units to deploy as you wish.

One interesting factor is the notion of the prevailing political attitude of the nation you're invading. If they have your same alignment—Populist, for instance—they fall easier and can only be occupied by one military unit. If, however, they have an opposing ideology or an entrenched military, it is much more difficult to defeat them, and many more units must be kept in the country to secure the peace. If you remove any of these units, a revolution occurs, and the country often goes to one of your opponents! This is worse than if you didn't conquer the country at all since you've wasted troops, and your enemy now has a foothold near you which was gained without any loss of strength. So make sure you don't spread yourself so thin that you can't keep the countries you conquer.

WinRisk

Who's It From? Steve Stancliff

Where Is It? X:\WINGAMES\
WINRISK

How Do I Use It? Run WINRISK in
Windows.

How Do I Order? Freeware

WinRisk is another general conquest game, much simpler to play than *Empire II* but no less challenging for that. The simplified interface and smaller number of units and countries involved makes for somewhat shorter games and simpler strategies, which means you can buzz through a world conquest more quickly. Still, it's pretty tricky at times.

In *WinRisk* you begin with a simplified map of the world colored in flat gray. Each country—you and two computer opponents—take turns claiming an area. After you divvy up the world, you can place extra units to strengthen certain positions and prepare to launch attacks on the others. Control is simply a matter of mouse clicks: left click on the number box to place new units in a country, left click to choose a country to attack from and then a country to attack, right click to transfer units from one of your countries to another to strengthen a border. Easy.

Still, this can be a pretty tricky game. I found myself groaning as ownership of certain countries swayed back and forth, the computer always seeming to have the upper hand. (I suspect it cheats, but then almost all AIs do.) It doesn't require a lot to play a game of *WinRisk*, which makes it a perfect little wargame for when your brain is out to lunch. Just click away and watch the crazy seesaw of country ownership change from your own red to bright lime green to an ominous navy blue. Have at it.

Oh, and don't worry about registering this one: it's freeware, no doubt because of trademark problems.

The "Battles" Series

Who's It From? Glacier Edge Technology

Where Is It? X:\WINGAMES\WWII & BDD & BDP

How Do I Use It? Run WWII, BDD, or BDP in Windows.

What Do I Get? An introductory scenario.

What Am I Missing? More scenarios.

How Much? See below.

How Do I Order? Glacier Edge Technology, 4820 East Kentucky Ave., Ste. E, Glendale, CO 80222.

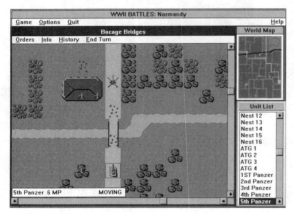

Beginning with *Battles on Distant Planets*, and continuing with *Battles on Distant Deserts* and *World War II Battles*, Glacier Edge has brought a series of simple, mouse-driven wargames to the Windows environment. They're easy to get into, and feature a pretty wide degree of control and a good variety of units and locations.

World War II Battles: As was proven with the recent commemorations for the 50th anniversary of D-Day, we still have a fascination with the massive effort which led to the liberation of Europe. Wargamers are drawn to the beaches known as Utah, Omaha, Gold, Juno, and Sword by the what-ifs: what if the landings had not been as successful, what if Hitler had unleashed his panzers, what if air and naval support had not weakened the enemy? What if, indeed.

Glacier Edge's *World War II Battles: The Bocage Bridges* is a squad-level simulation of the American and German clash over some key bridges spanning a Normandy river. Squad level is one of the smallest levels a wargamer can successfully manage, but because it involves minute control of many units over a limited space, it isn't always popular. (*Squad Leader* is the best-known game of this type.) A squad is comprised of about eight to ten men, armed with rifles, under a single leader, or a single tank, mortar, anti-tank, or machine-gun unit.

The main flaws of *WWII Battles* lay in its garish green terrain colors (something more muted would have been preferable), and the simple fact that managing a

---

WWII Tips

If you play as the Americans in WWII Battles, you have to rush for the bridges, sweeping the enemy aside or simply bypassing them. As the Germans, you have to prevent the Americans from getting to the bridges. Terrain includes the thick "bocage:" the tangled "walls" of stone and vegetation that choke the countryside and prevent free movement. The Germans can use the terrain to setup ambushes, and dodging these ambushes will be the most difficult task facing the Americans. Americans should mass tanks and infantry into several spearheads to effectively deal with this threat.

---

squad-level game is always a bit tricky and requires patient shuttling of troops across the map. That and the fact that infantry icons look like eight ants grouped together mean there's room for improvement, but it's still a good, playable system.

Registration and the additional scenarios "The Armored Hedgerows," "The General," and "A Last Stand" can be had for $33.

Battles on Distant Deserts: The same system used for *WWII* is used effectively here for some hypothetical Gulf War scenarios. You again control squad-level units (including some choppers) in a series of missions, this time across a desert landscape. Beginning with "Berm Busting," you have to either hit Saddam's dug-in units (as the Americans) or defend your berms against attack (as the Iraqis). The stark desert sands mean the graphics can be somewhat monotonous at times, but the shading on the units and other terrain features are quite nicely executed.

"The Streets of Kahfji" and "Road to Al Zibayir" can be had, along with registration, for a mere $23.

Battles on Distant Planets: This was the first of Glacier Edges "Battle" games and has remained a perennial shareware favorite. *BDP* offers science-fiction scenarios set on far-flung worlds. The units, though futuristically styled, are basically the equivalents of infantry, air, chopper, and armor squads. The first scenario, which you have here, is "Night on Rancor," and centers around the ongoing fight between the Knoll and the Terrans.

"Desert Counter-Attack," "The Princess," and "Netherworld" scenarios can all be ordered for $43.

X-COM

Who's It From? MicroProse Software

Where Is It? X:\DOSDEMO\XCOM

How Do I Use It? Type XCOM at the DOS prompt

What Do I Get? Interactive demo

How Much? $49.95

How Do I Order? MicroProse Entertainment Software, 180 Lakefront Dr., Hunt Valley, MD 21030. (410) 771-1151.

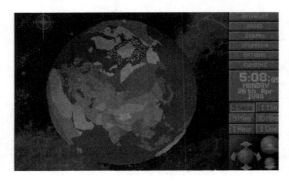

As you've been reading along in this chapter, you've probably noticed something: that a preponderance of brilliant strategy games seems to flow from MicroProse as from no other company. With *X-COM*, MicroProse's U.K. division has hit on one of its most unusual and unique ideas. Loosely based on the 1970s television series *UFO*—a cult fave—*X-COM* posits a planet Earth, late in the 1990s, that is the scene of steadily escalating UFO activity. Sightings, abductions, landings, and even attacks are growing world wide, and to deal with the threat, the UN establishes the Extraterrestrial Combat Unit (X-COM). Funded by countries around the globe to the tune of $16 million a year, X-COM is charged with immediately responding to UFO sightings and threats.

You are the head of X-COM, with the power to establish bases anywhere in the world, send ships to chase down UFOs, order strike teams into crash sites and alien bases to battle the invaders, buy weapons and equipment, and conduct research on aliens, alien weapons, and new technology for your troops. In short, you have total control over the war against the aliens.

The design of *X-COM* is so thoroughly thought-out and effective that it makes getting into the complex elements of the game relatively easy. (A task made even easier by a series of good tutorials.) The main screen is centered around a globe which can be zoomed and rotated along any axis. You begin by placing your first base, then start the ever-running game clock (in any number of time increments from 5 minutes to one day) and wait for a sighting. When one is reported, you send a fighter ship to shoot it down, and then a strike team to investigate the wreckage. Once the strike team reaches its destination, the view changes to a

X-COM ALIEN MISSIONS

Just what are those damn aliens doing on Earth anyway? Here's a list of the alien missions and what they mean.

Research   Generally harmless missions using small vehicles in remote areas. The least threat.

Harvest   Harvesters abduct cattle and may mutilate them to extract various organs for their own purposes. Very disturbing to governments.

Abduction   Abductors will snatch human subjects and submit them to horrible experiments. This causes governments great alarm.

Infiltration   Human-like aliens infiltrate governments, signing pacts which allow them to operate unhindered in that country. They'll also make the government withdraw from the X-Com Project. The pacts are signed on a battleship and result in detrimental loss of contributing countries and a corresponding decrease in funds.

Base   Aliens will attempt to build underground bases in remote locations to serve as command centers for further alien operations. Two supply ships and a battleship will be needed to establish the base, and each base must be resupplied once a month. Bases may contain an alien commander. Disturbs governments.

Terror   Aliens will will use a "terror ship" to frighten the populace, creating "terror sites."

Retaliation   If you're doing well, expect a battleship to attack one of your bases. This is the most dangerous alien operation for X-COM.

Supply   Supply ships restock alien bases once a month. The best way to locate a base is to follow a supply ship.

X-COM ALIENS

Alien Races: More than one alien race is unleashing their diabolical plans on the earth. In the course of *X-COM*, you'll come across five major alien races, each with one or more "drones" that accompany them. They have different characteristics, and some are more dangerous than others. Here's a rundown of what to expect.

Sectoid   Though these aliens are frail and weak, they have a psi ability that can turn your own troops against you. Don't underestimate them.

Cyberdiscs accompany the Sectoids. They're resilient, well-armed, and float. Their Achilles' heel? They can be manipulated with psi into firing at themselves. When they die, they sometimes explode, taking out everything around them.

Floater   Though they can fly, Floaters also have low-armor and no psi abilities, making them fairly easy to dispatch. Mostly used for terror missions.

Reapers may look like toads, but their large jaws are like steel traps, and they can shred armor as easily as they can civilians. Like Floaters, they are most effective at terrorizing the populace.

Snakeman   The Snakemen are well-armored but have no special skills, abilities, or attacks. They derive their strike strength from their drones, the Chryssalids.

skewed, 3D top down view of the terrain. Deployment of troops, recon of the area, and combat with aliens occurs in rounds, and each soldier has certain movement and health values. The goal is to effectively use your troops to kill all the aliens and return them to the lab for dissection. Not an easy task! They're better armed and smarter, and you'll face some tough opposition and suffer quite a few deaths as you fight the intruders.

Chryssalids kill with a touch and are lightning quick. Their claws can destroy the heaviest tanks instantly, but they usually don't use them on people. Instead, they inject strike teams with eggs a la *Alien*. The infected members of the team become zombified, and, when injured, bloom into full-grown Chryssalids. At terror sites, they do this to civilians and make the clean-up job well-nigh impossible. Fear them.

Muton These are good shots and pack a mean plasma gun. They'll take out some weaker operatives with a single hit.

Celatids can find anyone anywhere. Once found, these floaters will fire a powerful, though often inaccurate, venom.

Silacoids are slow-moving eating machines that can digest metal as easily as they can your squad. Hard to avoid in tight quarters, but fairly vulnerable to attack.

Ethereal These eggheads are your worst nightmare. Though physically the weakest race, they have the highest psi rating, and can often wield the powers of other races and unleash a withering psionic blast. Their dark cloaks act as a type of super-armor, protecting their frail bodies from attack. They move fast and shoot accurately.

Sectopods are strong units with practically unstoppable firepower and the highest armor ratings of any unit. Any but the extremely well-armed and armored can forget about living through an encounter with these aliens.

X-COM involves many disparate facets—combat, strategy, base-building, research, production, and resource management—yet weaves them all together into a completely manageable and totally engrossing game.

Master of Orion

Who's It From? MicroProse/SimTex

Where Is It? X:\DOSDEMO\ORION

How Do I Use It? Copy to hard drive and type INSTALL at the DOS prompt.

What Do I Get? Non-interactive demo.

How Much? $47.95

How Do I Order? MicroProse Entertainment Software, 180 Lakefront Dr., Hunt Valley, MD 21030-2245. (410) 771-1151.

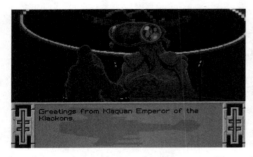
Greetings from Klaquan Emperor of the Klackons.

If you keep up with computer gaming, you couldn't help but notice that 1994 was the year of the space-strategy game. It seemed as though a new one showed up every month, but one of the first and certainly still the best is *Master of Orion*. Though based around a completely different structure, it immediately calls to mind *Civilization*, in no small part because you begin with only one planet and limited resources, and must manage the growth of technology, exploration, expansion of the military, espionage, research, industry, and ecology. Meanwhile, you're looking for new planets to explore and trying to position yourself against or ally yourself with any one of nine other alien races.

Though these similarities to the substance of *Civilization* are marked, the game has quite a different feel. First, how you play and what "edge" you have on the opponents is gauged by what race you choose to be. The Sakkra, for example, reproduce at a high rate and can overwhelm with sheer numbers, while the Psilons excel at science and research. Each race has a skill area where it has an advantage, and as you play as the different races, you'll find strategy and gameplay altering to suit that advantage.

You can play in any size universe, from small to huge, with each one featuring more planets to explore and conquer. Up to five other aliens can compete against you for the same galaxy, and each one will need to be dealt with in a different way. You begin by developing your planet's economic resources and building a fleet to colonize other planets, leapfrogging from one to another. As your technology levels grow, you can build better and better space ships, from light fighters to heavy battlecruisers. You can pursue diplomacy and trade with your enemies, or simply smash them into a raw pulp, but the ultimate goal is to reach and conquer the planet Orion. Populated ages ago by an elder race of superior power and intelligence, Orion is guarded by a computer-controlled ship. The would-be master of the galaxy must defeat this ship and successfully conquer Orion. No mean feat.

If you only buy one galaxy-spanning conquest game, it should be *Master of Orion*, simply because it has the most depth, the widest range of possible approaches, and unbeatable replayability.

Master of Magic

Who's It From? MicroProse/SimTex	**How Much?** $57.95
Where Is It? X:\DOSDEMO\MAGIC	**How Do I Order?** MicroProse Enter-
How Do I Use It? Type MAGIC at the DOS prompt.	tainment Software, 180 Lakefront Dr., Hunt Valley, MD 21030-2245. (410) 771-1151.
What Do I Get? Interactive demo.	

What could SimTex do to follow up on the popular *Master of Orion*? Why, *Master of Magic*, which seeks to be to fantasy/strategy gaming what *MOO* is to science-fiction/strategy gaming, while at the same time being completely different. Does it work? You bet.

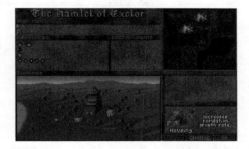

The game *MOM* most resembles isn't *Master of Orion* but *Civilization*: a comparison that's abundantly clear from the first few screens. You begin by choosing one of fourteen wizards as your character (much like you chose leaders in *Civilization*), or creating your own. This character will specialize in an area of magic, and imbue various character traits, such as Aggressive, Peaceful, Expansionist, and so on. Your wizard is given a small city to develop and some magical units to explore the realm, pushing back the blackness which engulfs all unknown territory. You must explore not only the main world, but also a dark, alternate world of myriad races and creatures of all kinds. Settlers go forth to found new cities, and army units go out to conquer existing ones.

To help you keep a finger on the status of your kingdom, you have a bevy of advisors for everything from taxes and mapping to astrology, and a magical apprentice. On the city map, you can upgrade structures and build new ones, such as an

Alchemist's Guild, Fantastic Stable, or War College. Either workers or farmers dwell in these cities, producing the goods and food needed for your empire to grow. As you researched technology in both *Master of Orion* and *Civilization*, so you research new and ever more powerful spells in *MOM*. Along the way, you can send heroes out on special quests, encounter new races and creatures, and forge elaborate diplomatic ties. When it comes time for battle, opposing units meet in a skewed, top-down view of the combat field. With some impressive pyrotechnics, they hurl spells at each other in a fight to the death.

Other games have tried, and succeeded, at this style of game before. Most notably, *Warlords II*, *Stronghold*, and *Fantasy Empires* were successful blends of magic and empire building. But *Master of Magic* ups the stakes by allowing so much control over the management of the empire and providing so much depth in terms of units, magic, combat, construction, and just about every other area.

1944: Across the Rhine

Who's It From? MicroProse

Where Is It? X:\DOSDEMO\1944ATR

How Do I Use It? Type ATR at the DOS prompt.

What Do I Get? Non-interactive demo.

How Much? $57.95

How Do I Order? MicroProse Entertainment Software, 180 Lakefront Dr., Hunt Valley, MD 21030-2245. (410) 771-1151.

I'm at a bit of a disadvantage in discussing *Across the Rhine* because, as I write this, I haven't seen anything of it but this demo and a few articles! Still, considering MicroProse's reputation for sims and the early scuttlebutt, most notably from historian and game journalist William Trotter, this game looks like it could be hot. *Across the Rhine* puts you right in both Allies and Axis tanks during the heavy armored battles for Europe during World War II: something that has *never* been done effectively before. You can play individual scenarios or a campaign game, beginning with D-Day and going right up to the end of the war. There are even hypothetical scenarios, which start you in some location and challenge you to create the strategy that will lead to victory or defeat. You can command any level from platoon to battalion, and be of any rank you desire. You can take on as much or as little responsibility as you like. Want to just hop in and drive the tanks? No problem! Want to make strategic decisions? Go for it! There is also a wide variety of tank types to choose from on both sides, and enough options to keep play fresh for some time. If *ATR* fulfills its promise, it could be the best tank game ever. Keep your fingers crossed.

1942: Pacific Air War

Who's It From? MicroProse

Where Is It? X:\DOSDEMO\1942PAW

How Do I Use It? Type RUNME at the DOS prompt.

What Do I Get? Non-interactive demo.

How Much? $59.95

How Do I Order? MicroProse Entertainment Software, 180 Lakefront Dr., Hunt Valley, MD 21030-2245. (410) 771-1151.

I have always been fascinated with the War in the Pacific during World War II—the crucible in which much of what we now regard as modern warfare was refined. From the largest naval battles ever fought, to the planes which threaded through flak-filled skies to sink their teeth into the enemy, it was a time of grand triumph and bitter tragedy. Everything about it was epic.

The first time I played *Aces of the Pacific* from Dynamix, I was hooked. I flew mission after mission as both Americans and Japanese, starting several careers and going down in flames several times. For the first time, I actually felt like I could experience a small piece of this war, albeit only in the faintest way. When MicroProse turned its formidable flight sim skills to this theater, I was looking forward to it, but I was also dubious. How could anyone improve upon *Aces*?

I should have known. Technology moves on, and while *Aces* is still a terrific sim, *1942: Pacific Air War* has eclipsed it not only with unbelievably good graphics, but with the ability to control carrier movements during battle!

Everything you'd expect from this kind of a game is here and more. You can play individual missions, or launch a career that will (hopefully) take you through the war. There are powerful mission recording functions, great exterior views, a fully panning "virtual cockpit" the likes of which has never been seen before, great flight models, and some of the best graphics *ever* seen in a flight sim! Some small flaws in the released versions are hardly an issue: the time compress function isn't as efficient as the one in *Aces*, and the sound effects are marginal. But so many elements are so well-executed that even these points fail to bother me. With a new CD-ROM version due out featuring new missions, interviews with veterans, new graphics, and a rumored modem play mode, it's clear that *PAW* will be around for some time, as it deserves to be.

☆ Falcon 3.0/Falcon Gold ☆

Who's It From? Spectrum HoloByte

Where Is It? X:\DOSDEMO\FALCON3

How Do I Use It? Type FALCON3 at the DOS prompt.

What Do I Get? Interactive demo.

How Much? $69.95

How Do I Order? Spectrum HoloByte, 2490 Mariner Square Loop, Alameda, CA 94501.

Before *Falcon*, flight simulators were just games. *Falcon*'s rallying call was "realism," and Spectrum HoloByte believed that people would stick with the game through a steep learning curve in order for that extra pay-off. They did, and *Falcon 3.0* became *the* flight simulator against which all others were measured.

Since the initial release of *Falcon 3.0*, Spectrum HoloByte has expanded on it and their "Electronic Battlefield Series" with several stellar add-ons and stand-alone products. *Operation: Fighting Tiger*, *MiG 29*, and *Hornet: Naval Strike Fighter* added new aircraft and new theaters of war, creating the single best unified flight sim series in gaming history. Now, all of these classic games, along with some extras, are included in the attractively priced *Falcon Gold*. Bringing *Falcon* to CD-ROM would have been noteworthy in itself, but creating such a jam-packed disk makes this the best flight sim package ever released to CD-ROM.

The heart of *Falcon Gold* is, of course, Falcon itself. Putting the user in the cockpit of an F-16 air superiority jet in the enemy-laden skies of Kuwait, Panama, and Israel, *Falcon* offers the best dogfighting action available anywhere. Though it

THE PLANES OF *FALCON GOLD*

F-16 "Fighting Falcon"

Type:	Air superiority fighter
Manufacturer:	General Dynamics
Top speed:	Mach 2
Maximum range:	2,415 nm
Combat radius:	500 nm
Ceiling:	60,000 feet
Arms:	20mm six-barrel cannon
	Wingtip mounts (for air-to-air missiles)
	9 hardpoints carrying 15,200 lbs. of other stores

F/A-18 "Hornet"

Type:	Carrier based multi-role fighter
Manufacturer:	McDonnell Douglas
Top speed:	Mach 1.8
Maximum range:	2,000 nm
Combat radius:	550 nm
Ceiling:	50,000 feet
Arms:	20 mm cannon
	9 hardpoints carrying 17,000 lbs. of other stores

MiG-29 "Fulcrum"

Type:	Multi-role fighter
Manufacturer:	Mikoyan-Gurevich
Top speed:	Mach 2.3
Maximum range:	1,130 nm
Combat radius:	400 nm
Ceiling:	56,000 feet
Weight (min/max):	25,000/42,500 lbs.
Arms:	30 mm cannon
	6 hardpoints carrying 8,500 lbs. of other stores

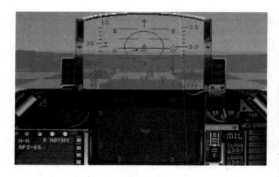

comes with numerous difficulty settings, allowing users as much or as little realism as they desire, this is still a tough plane to fly, and requires patience and many hours of practice. The payoff for this investment of time and effort is the most realistic play available in any flight sim. Numerous training exercises, instant action, unified campaigns in which you direct an entire squadron of fighters, intelligent wingmen, and both modem and network play makes this a truly full-featured game. If you run out of missions, *Falcon Gold* also includes all of *Operation Fighting Tiger*, featuring new mission types, new weapons, and new theaters of war (Southeast Asia, India, and the Far East).

While flying the F-16, you're bound to run across more than a few Russian-built MiG-29s. Well, now it's time to fly one. *MiG-29* creates an entirely new flight model, putting you on the other side of the guns in one the most responsive planes in the sky. With an unbelievable climb rate, tight turning radius, infrared weapon tracking, aiming monocle, and auto-firing guns, the MiG-29 is almost more fun to fly than the F-16. You can now fly all the original *Falcon* missions as well as those in *Operation Fighting Tiger* from the other side, with missions in Iraq, Russia, Syria, Cuba, North Korea, and India. To round out the new flight models in this series, Spectrum HoloByte created *Hornet: Naval Strike Fighter*. This time, you're flying the F/A-18 Hornet for the U.S. Navy or Marines. The F/A-18, which excels as a ground-strike fighter, delivers carrier-based operations in all the series theaters of war, and adds the Balkan conflict as well.

As an added bonus, *Falcon Gold* also comes with *Art of the Kill*, a guide to effective fighter tactics. Featuring a book and on-disk video from ace trainer Pete Bonanni, *Art of the Kill* offers a series of effective lessons on how to improve your flight sim skills.

Falcon Gold requires at least 11 megs of hard drive space, with some additional space to play the video for *Art of the Kill*, but that's substantially less than all these games would take up without the CD. In addition, you get the latest version of all these sims, featuring bug fixes and improvements to the flight models of each. Altogether, this is the best single flight sim CD-ROM package you can get.

F-15 Strike Eagle III

Who's It From? MicroProse

Where Is It? X:\DOSDEMO\F15SE3

How Do I Use It? Type F15 at DOS prompt.

What Do I Get? Interactive demo.

How Much? $57.95

How Do I Order? MicroProse Entertainment Software, 180 Lakefront Dr., Hunt Valley, MD 21030-2245. (410) 771-1151.

Flight sim consumers come in two varieties: gamers who like to get into the air quickly and shoot at stuff, and air combat junkies who like *absolute* realism and *perfect* flight models that take *weeks* to master...so they can get into the air and shoot at stuff. F-15 Strike Eagle II catered to the former, while *F-15 Strike Eagle III* seeks to cater to both.

The original *Strike Eagle* games did not attempt to model all the nuances and intricacies of actual jet flight and combat. They were basically arcade games with an attitude, offering average consumers a feeling of realism without all the effort it takes to earn that realism. Spurred by the success of Spectrum HoloByte's *Falcon 3.0*, which at its most complex levels offers the most realistic flight models available outside of mega-million dollar military training devices, MicroProse pushed the envelope when developing the latest installment of its most popular simulator. Realism became the new goal: they were going to do for the F-15 what Falcon did for the F-16. Since these two planes are radically different in design and purpose, the result would—in theory—be a complement to Falcon. But in the small world of jet combat sims, comparisons are unavoidable.

The actual F-15 has been through several design overhauls since its introduction in the early '70s, the most recent being the F-15E, upon which *Strike Eagle III* is modeled. It was a sharp turn for the F-15 toward a two-seater ground-strike jet that retains its proven air-to-air capabilities. Improved avionics and the addition of a weapons systems officer (Wizzo) give the E-model the ability to penetrate enemy territory at very low altitudes and neutralize targets quickly and efficiently. Unlike the nimble, single-engine F-16, which is primarily an air superiority fighter, the F-15E (dubbed the "Mud Eagle" for its low-altitude role) is a double-engine beast with a lethal air-to-ground payload and several tons more weight. Ergo, it is a bit less maneuverable in close-quarters combat.

So MicroProse is offering something slightly different in *Strike Eagle III*, leaning more on the strategy of air-to-ground missions than the flashy dogfighting of Falcon. Reality settings offer four generic categories from Easy to Extreme, but

each one of twelve options can be modified as either Standard or Authentic for such things as flight model, weapons effectiveness, displays, radar, etc. Some settings simplify the displays a bit or make the enemy slower to react, but on the whole the game doesn't simply become a arcade-type shoot-'em-up when settings are on standard: they just make the advanced mode seem more accurate and challenging. You start your career as a second lieutenant flying missions in Korea, the Persian Gulf, or Panama. Each theater offers its own challenges: the hills of Korea and Panama make low-flying a bit trickier but help mask the plane from radar, while the flat deserts of the Gulf offer no easy means of dodging a radar signal behind a mountain.

There is no arguing that *Strike Eagle III* is more attractive than *Falcon*. The shading and texturing, the bitmapped explosions, the terrain, and target detail are a far cry from Falcon's flat polygons. The Eagle itself is beautifully rendered, and weapons delivery simply looks better and more realistic than Falcon. Targets always explode with the same bitmapped graphic, but it's a fairly attractive one and better than what Falcon offers. After each flight, a "video" recap of the mission provides a slick replay of hits and misses without actually being useful.

But a flight sim is more than just good looks: it stands or falls on its flight model. The *Strike Eagle III* model is a vast improvement over version II. Handling is more unforgiving and payload weight affects maneuverability more accurately. Set to Authentic, the electronic warfare systems and weapons delivery modes are tricky to master but still accessible to most gamers who just want to get down to business. Finding the enemy, locking on the target, keeping your six clear, and dodging ground threats make this more difficult than your average sim, but still not the slave to realism that Falcon is. The result is an accessible yet realistic sim: an excellent addition to a crammed market.

Gunship 2000

Who's It From? MicroProse

Where Is It? X:\DOSDEMO\GUNSHIP

How Do I Use It? Type GSDEMO at the DOS prompt.

What Do I Get? Interactive demo.

How Much? $25.95

How Do I Order? MicroProse Entertainment Software, 180 Lakefront Dr., Hunt Valley, MD 21030-2245. (410) 771-1151.

By computer standards, *Gunship 2000* is a relic. One look at the polygon graphics and you'll either get nostalgic or just give up altogether, but one fact that remains unassailable is this: *Gunship 2000* is still the finest helicopter simulation ever released. No game in the almost four years since its release has come close. (And, yes, I especially mean *Comanche: Maximum Overkill*, which is an arcade game disguised as a sim.) On its hardest settings, this puppy ain't easy to fly, but once you do you'll be flying missions ranging from the jungles of Panama to the deserts of the Middle East to the frozen wastes of Antarctica. All enhancements and mission add-ons are now available on CD-ROM, and if you want to fly a helicopter sim, this is the way to go.

MANUFACTURER DIRECTORY AND PRODUCT LIST

21st Century Entertainment, P.O. Box 415, Webster, NY 14580. (716) 872-1200.
    Pinball Fantasies

Activision, 11601 Wilshire Blvd., 10th Floor, Los Angeles, CA 90025. (800) 477-3650.
    MechWarrior 2: The Clans
    Return to Zork

Allen, Geoff, 7232 Kananasjis Dr. SW, Calgary, Alberta, Canada T2V 2N2.
    Doom: The Real Thing

American Laser Games, 4801 Lincoln Rd. NE, Albuquerque, NM 87109. (505) 880-1718.
    Crime Patrol
    Space Pirates

Anderson, Nels, 92 Bishop Dr., Framingham, MA 01701-6515.
    Cipher for Windows

Apogee, 3960 Broadway, Suite 235, Garland, TX 75043. (800) APOGEE1.
    Blake Stone
    Halloween Harry
    Mystic Towers
    Raptor

AT-Ware, 720 Sunrise Ave., #28, Roseville, CA 95661-4815.
    Draw 5 Video Poker

Balewski, Ron, 412 E. Ridge St., Nanticoke, PA 18634-2915.
    Mah Jongg for Windows

Balogh, Stephen, PO Box 414, Caulfield East, Melbourne, Australia 3145.
    Pentominos

Bethesda Softworks, 1370 Picard Dr., Rockville, MD 20850.
    Terminator: Rampage
    The Elder Scrolls 1: Arena

Broderbund, 500 Redwood Blvd., Novato, CA 94948-6121.
    Myst

Cignoni, Giovanni & Paolo, Viale G. Amendola 39, 57025 Piombino LI, Italy
    WinFight

Di Troia, John, 5 Mt Pleasant St., Saugus, MA 01906.
  GopherIt!
  Bow and Arrow

Diversions Software, 966 Kramer Court, Aurora, CO 80010. CIS: 76450,3711.
  Prarie Dog Hunt
  Prarie Dog Hunt II: Judgement Day
  Voodoo Doll for Windows

Eidolon, 5716 Masholu Ave., Riverdale, NY 10471.
  Millenium Auction

Electronic Arts, 1450 Fashion Island Blvd., San Mateo, CA 94403.
  Theme Park

Emnu, Yutaka, 920-1, Hijaski-Hinatsuk, Tsukuba, Ibaraki, 305 Japan.
  EmPipe

Epic MegaGames, 3204 Tower Oaks Blvd., Ste. 410, Rockville, MD 20852.
(800) 972-7434.
  Castle of the Winds: Question of Vengeance
  Jill of the Jungle
  Kiloblaster
  Solar Winds
  Zone 66

FormGen Corp., 11 Holland Dr., Bolton, Ontario, Canada. (905) 857-0022.
  Spear of Destiny CD-ROM

Glacier Edge Technology, 4820 East Kentucky Ave., Ste. E, Glendale, CO 80222.
  Battles in Distant Deserts
  Battles on Distant Planets
  World War II Battles

Goble, Brian L., 2218 Franklin Ave. E., Seattle, WA 98102. goble@u.washington.edu.
  Adventures of MicroMan

Goldfayn, Oleg, 2489 East Third St., Brooklyn, NY 11223. CIS: 71202,2013.
  Atlantic City Blackjack

id Software, c/o StarPak, P.O. Box 1230, Greeley, CO 80632. (800) IDGAMES.
  Doom

Impressions Software, 7 Melrose Dr., Farmington, CT 06032.
  Detroit

Interplay Productions, 17922 Fitch Ave., Irvine, CA 92714, (800) INTERPLAY.
   Alone in the Dark 2
   Alone in the Dark
   Battle Chess CD-ROM
   Battle Chess 4000
   Blackthorne
   Castles II: Siege & Conquest
   The Lost Vikings
   Out of this World
   Star Trek: 25th Anniversary CD-ROM
   Stark Trek: Judgment Rites

IntraCorp. Inc., Airport Corporate Center, 7200 Corporate Center Dr., Ste. 500, Miami, FL 33126. (800) 468-7226.
   Corridor 7: Alien Invasion

Ishi Press International, 76 Bonaventura Dr., San Jose, CA 95130. (408) 944-9900.
   IGO

Jarrett, Eric, P.O. Box 34749 , Richmond, VA 23234.
   Hangem

Junod, John A., 3005C Greene Place, West Point, NY 10996.
   Spider Solitaire

LucasArts Games, P.O. Box 10307, San Rafael, CA 94912. (800) STAR WARS.
   Day of the Tentacle
   Indiana Jones and the Fate of Atlantis
   Rebel Assault
   Sam & Max Hit the Road
   TIE Fighter
   X-Wing

McAuliffe, Michael, P.O. Box 3452, Reno, NV 89505. CIS: 70216,303.
   Stellar Warrior

Medeiros, Carlos, P.O. Box 4219, Fall River, MA 02722.
   Civilization Editor

Maxis, 2 Theatre Square, Orinda, CA 94563-3346.
   SimCity 2000

MicroProse Entertainment Software, 180 Lakefront Dr., Hunt Valley, MD 21030-2245.
(410) 771-1151.
  1942: Pacific Air War
  1944: Across the Rhine
  Civilization
  David Leadbetter's Greens
  DragonSphere
  F-15 Strike Eagle III
  Gunship 2000
  Master of Magic
  Master of Orion
  Railroad Tycoon Deluxe
  SubWar 2050
  Ultimate NFL Coaches Club Football
  World Circuit
  X-COM

Neto, Oscar Daudt, Rua Sebastiao Lacerda, 30/905-1, 22.240 Rio de Janeiro, Brazil.
  Amnesia

New World Computing, P.O. Box 4302, Hollywood, CA 90078-4302.
  Empire Deluxe

Nokleberg, Chris, 4315 Norris Rd., Fremont, CA 94536.
  Watch Out Willi!

Origin Systems, 12940 Research Blvd., Austin, TX 78750. (800) 245-4525.
  Shadowcaster
  System Shock
  Ultima Underworld

Pixel Publishers, P.O. Box 2847, Marrifield, VA 22116. (703) 222-0568.
  Xatax

Playdoe Entertainment Software, 2412 Desert Oak Dr., Palmdale, CA 93550.
  Quatra Command

Pop Software, P.O. Box 60995, Sunnyvale, CA 94088. (408) 450-3022; CIS: 71460,2432.
  Invasion of the Mutant Space Bats of Doom

Puraty, Dan, 3536 Kent Rd., Stow, OH 44224-4602. CIS: 71563,1245.
  Double Match
  Spin 'n' Win

Pyramid Software Development, 2651 Sunset Blvd., #903, Rocklin, CA 95677-4242.
Casino Twenty-One

Shadoware, P.O. Box 0155, New Port Richey, FL 34656-0155.
Dominate

Shikoh, Alan, 1421 Briarcliff Ave., Charlottesville, VA 22903. (804) 979-0378.
Brainteaser

Sierra On-Line, P.O. Box 53250, Bellevue, WA 98015-3250. (800) 757-7707.
Freddy Pharkas: Frontier Pharmacist
Front Page Sports: Baseball
Gabriel Knight: The Sins of the Fathers
Lode Runner: The Legend Returns

Sofia Systems, P.O. Box 360188, Milpitas, CA 95036. (408) 942-5401.
Jpuzzle

Software Creations, 26 Harris St., Clinton, MA 01540. (508) 368-8654.
Jetpack
Crime Trivia
Hexxagon

SouthBay Software, P.O. Box 871, Torrance, CA 90508. Phone/Fax: 310-320-0614.
CIS: 70564,3210.
Runner

Spectrum HoloByte, 2490 Mariner Square Loop, Alameda, CA 94501. (800) 695-GAME.
BreakThru
Falcon 3.0
Falcon Gold

SSI, 675 Almanor Ave., Ste. 201, Sunnyvale, CA 94086-2901. (800) 245-4525.
CyClones
Dark Legions
Menzoberranzan
Flashback
Ravenloft

Stanley, John Dee, 6959 California Ave. SW, Seattle, WA 98136.
Megatron

Sutty, George, 79006 Moonmist Circle, Huntington Beach, CA 92647.
Backgammon

Tagliaferri, Matt, 4416 Brooklyn Ave., Cleveland, OH 44109.
  DoomCAD

Thomas, Daniel, 2301 North Huron Circle, Placentia, CA 92670. CIS: 72301,2174.
Prodigy: CWRF01A.
  Canfield for Windows

Timberline Software, 12558 W. Aqueduct Dr., Littleton, CO 80127-6225.
CIS: 71162,2761.
  Destroyer for Windows

van der Loeff, Arnod, Wilhelminastraat 159-3, 1054 WD Amsterdam, The Netherlands.
  TurboGo

Velocity Development, P.O. Box 2749, San Franciso, CA 94126.
  Spectre VR

Viable Software Alternatives, Route 10, Box 360, Carbondale, IL 62901.
  Empire II for Windows

Wicked Witch Software Company, P.O. Box 3452, Reno, NV 89505.
  Bandit

Zamzow, Dean, 1171 Cordelia Ave., San Jose, CA 95129.
  Windows Video Poker

INDEX

Note to the Reader

Boldfaced numbers indicate pages where you will find the principal discussion of a topic or the definition of a term.

GET A FREE CATALOG JUST FOR EXPRESSING YOUR OPINION.

Help us improve our books and get a *FREE* full-color catalog in the bargain. Please complete this form, pull out this page and send it in today. The address is on the reverse side.

Name _____   **Company** _____

Address _____   **City** _____ **State** ____ **Zip** _____

Phone ( )_____

1. How would you rate the overall quality of this book?

- ❑ Excellent
- ❑ Very Good
- ❑ Good
- ❑ Fair
- ❑ Below Average
- ❑ Poor

2. What were the things you liked most about the book? (Check all that apply)

- ❑ Pace
- ❑ Format
- ❑ Writing Style
- ❑ Examples
- ❑ Table of Contents
- ❑ Index
- ❑ Price
- ❑ Illustrations
- ❑ Type Style
- ❑ Cover
- ❑ Depth of Coverage
- ❑ Fast Track Notes

3. What were the things you liked *least* about the book? (Check all that apply)

- ❑ Pace
- ❑ Format
- ❑ Writing Style
- ❑ Examples
- ❑ Table of Contents
- ❑ Index
- ❑ Price
- ❑ Illustrations
- ❑ Type Style
- ❑ Cover
- ❑ Depth of Coverage
- ❑ Fast Track Notes

4. Where did you buy this book?

- ❑ Bookstore chain
- ❑ Small independent bookstore
- ❑ Computer store
- ❑ Wholesale club
- ❑ College bookstore
- ❑ Technical bookstore
- ❑ Other _____

5. How did you decide to buy this particular book?

- ❑ Recommended by friend
- ❑ Recommended by store personnel
- ❑ Author's reputation
- ❑ Sybex's reputation
- ❑ Read book review in _____
- ❑ Other _____

6. How did you pay for this book?

- ❑ Used own funds
- ❑ Reimbursed by company
- ❑ Received book as a gift

7. What is your level of experience with the subject covered in this book?

- ❑ Beginner
- ❑ Intermediate
- ❑ Advanced

8. How long have you been using a computer?

years _____

months _____

9. Where do you most often use your computer?

- ❑ Home
- ❑ Work

- ❑ Both
- ❑ Other _____

10. What kind of computer equipment do you have? (Check all that apply)

- ❑ PC Compatible Desktop Computer
- ❑ PC Compatible Laptop Computer
- ❑ Apple/Mac Computer
- ❑ Apple/Mac Laptop Computer
- ❑ CD ROM
- ❑ Fax Modem
- ❑ Data Modem
- ❑ Scanner
- ❑ Sound Card
- ❑ Other _____

11. What other kinds of software packages do you ordinarily use?

- ❑ Accounting
- ❑ Databases
- ❑ Networks
- ❑ Apple/Mac
- ❑ Desktop Publishing
- ❑ Spreadsheets
- ❑ CAD
- ❑ Games
- ❑ Word Processing
- ❑ Communications
- ❑ Money Management
- ❑ Other _____

12. What operating systems do you ordinarily use?

- ❑ DOS
- ❑ OS/2
- ❑ Windows
- ❑ Apple/Mac
- ❑ Windows NT
- ❑ Other _____

13. On what computer-related subject(s) would you like to see more books?

_____

_____

_____

_____

14. Do you have any other comments about this book? (Please feel free to use a separate piece of paper if you need more room)

_____

_____

_____

_____

- - - - - - - - - - - PLEASE FOLD, SEAL, AND MAIL TO SYBEX - - - - - - - - - - -

SYBEX INC.
Department M
2021 Challenger Drive
Alameda, CA
94501

ABOUT THE AUTHOR

In addition to being a Contributing Editor and Columnist for *PC Gamer*, *CD-ROM Today*, *Computer Entertainment News*, and *Cemetery Dance* magazines, T. Liam McDonald's articles, reviews, and stories have appeared in *Game Player PC Entertainment*, *Atlantic City*, *The Fine Art of Murder*, *Armchair Detective*, *Shivers*, *BookPage*, *Cut!*, *Computer Gaming World*, *The Thomas Wolfe Review*, and numerous other publications. After working for years in the film and television industry, he started writing full time, and has published over 150 reviews, articles, and stories, most in the computer and computer entertainment field. His books include *The 11th Hour/7th Guest Companion* (forthcoming from SYBEX Inc.), *Shadowplays*, *Sea-Cursed*, and *Sun Tzu's Ancient Art of Golf*.

USING THE DISC

- The entries in this book refer to files on the free CD-ROM bound onto the opposite page. These entries provide the location of the various games, as well as startup and operating instructions. If you have trouble running any title, please refer to its entry.

- With the wide variety of system configurations and memory issues, there are bound to be titles that simply don't work, or don't work smoothly, on some machines. The minimum system requirement for many is a 386/40 with 4 MB of RAM and at least 580K free conventional memory. Many others *won't work* without a 486/33 with 8 MB of RAM, expanded memory (see the introduction), or, in several cases, a SoundBlaster (or compatible) sound card. Most demos that have sound will support a SoundBlaster set to either IRQ 5 or 7. Some demos may not support your sound card, and may lock up or run without sound.

- The titles on this CD-ROM are completely unzipped, and many can be run straight from the disk! However, most weren't optimized for CD-ROM, and there may be some performance degradation. We have found several titles that worked poorly, or not at all, on some systems when used straight from the CD-ROM. These are *Blake Stone, Bow and Arrow, BreakThru, Castle of the Winds, Dominate, Double Match, Empire II, Master of Orion, Menzoberranzan, Lode Runner, Quatra, Runner, Shadowcaster, Spin n Win, TIE Fighter, Ultima Underworld, Watch Out Willi!,* and *Prairie Dog Hunt,* and they should be copied to the hard drive before using. If a game is giving you some trouble, try copying it to the hard drive, running SOUND or INSTALL, or optimizing your memory.

- Some Windows titles require that certain files be in your X:\WINDOWS\SYSTEM directory. These files are on the CD-ROM under the X:\WINFILES directory, and should be copied over to the X:\WINDOWS\SYSTEM directory if you encounter any trouble with Windows games.

- At least one title, *Millenium Auction,* requires Video for Windows. To load Video for Windows, run SETUP in the X:\WINGAMES\WINVIDEO directory.

- To use a title in DOS, change to your CD-ROM drive by typing X:, where X: is the name of the drive. (This protocol is used throughout the book.) Access the game's subdirectory by typing CD [DIRECTORY NAME] (ie, CD XWING). Check the entry for the executable file for that title and enter it at the DOS prompt. Windows games can be used either through the File Manager or the Run command. See the Introduction for further information about running games.

- If you encounter problems in running a title, please search the directory for files labeled README or with *.TXT or *.DOC extensions. Files with these extensions often provide information on ordering a particular game or fixing problems, so please check them out. Also look for *.BAT and *.EXE files and try running these if you're having trouble getting a title to work.

- And please remember: these are only demos. They may run slowly or without sound, they may crash without reason or not work at all depending on your system. They're free and only meant to give you a taste of a title, so you can decide whether to go out and buy it. Please take that into consideration when trying to run them.